Hope you enjoy it, too!

ISBN 0 85116 577-X

Printed and published in Great Britain by D. C. Thomson & Co., Ltd., 185 Fleet Street, London EC4A 2HS.

£4.35

welcome —

to the 1995 Mandy Annual. It's burstin' with groovy goodies. Get stuck in!

FAVES!

Write down some of the best bits.

FAVE STORY ....

MOST FABSY FEATURE ....

HUNKIEST POP STAR ....

CUTE 'N' CUDDLIEST THING ....

IT REALLY MADE ME LAUGH ....

THAT WAS DEAD SAD ....

EXCELLENT INTERESTING BIT ....

Penny's Place
PENNY JORDAN'S parents ran the "Penny's Place" café. Penny and her pals went to Chesterford High. One day, at school —
Attention, all those who wish to go on the school ski-ing trip to the French Alps. We shall want your payments by next Monday.
The ski-ing trip! I can't wait!
I have never skied. What is it like, Gemma?
Brilliant, Sita! You'll *LOVE* it!
I know *I* will. I've always wanted to have a go!
Later, in the café —
My Dad says he'll treat us all to a trip to the dry ski slopes on Saturday, so that we can get in some practice.
Not much point *ME* going, is there, Gemma?
Oh! Poor Donna. I hadn't even thought! Of course her folks won't be able to afford for her to go!

Well, come to the dry slopes with us anyway, Donna. It'll be good fun.
I suppose so.
Big deal!
So —
Ouch! It's harder than it looks!
Ha! Ha!
Arlene was an instant expert —
Whee! I can't wait to get to the mountains and try this for real!
It just isn't fair. I'm as good as the rest of them. But I'll never get NEAR a mountain. There's eight of us kids and Pa's out of work.
The day of departure came —
Poor Donna. It just doesn't seem right to leave her behind, Sita.
AND she'll have to do schoolwork while we're on holiday. She really does get all the rough luck, Penny.
Donna was miserable —
They'll be halfway to France right now — and I'm stuck doing rotten maths for Misery Miller.
Donna Green, pay attention! You are NOT on holiday!

She doesn't have to rub it in, the old moan! You're from 2B, aren't you? I'm Mike. What's your name?
Donna.
And in France —
This is our chalet, girls.
It's beautiful, miss.
Just one thing missing, or hadn't you noticed? Where's the snow?
Welcome to the Chalet St Michel. We hope for a snowfall very soon. In the meantime, there will unfortunately be no ski-ing.
We could've worked THAT one out!
Later —
Huh! I didn't come all this way just to go hill-walking!
But it's so beautiful here, Arlene! And, anyway, it beats being at school, doesn't it?
Agreed!
That evening, at the chalet —
Brrr! It's freezing in here! And what's happened to the lights?
We are most sorry. There has been a power cut. We have, however, prepared for you the dinner, to the best of our ability.

SALAD!
Brr! Lovely! J-just what we need! And if we're lucky maybe it'll be ice-cream for afters!
Shut up, Arlene! We're all cold enough already!
Then, later —
Look! SNOW! It's started SNOWING! We can ski tomorrow!
Hurray!
But, next morning —
We have outside the blizzard conditions. Today, you will have to stay in.
Aw, NO!
It had snowed in Chesterford, too. At Donna's —
Wanna play snowballs!
An' build a snowman!
Me too! Me too!
Take 'em to the park with you, Donna. They're getting under my feet!
So —
My pals will be having a brill time, and I'm stuck here with —
HEY!

Sorry, Donna! I couldn't resist it!
Oh, yeah?
Well, neither can I! Take *THAT!*
Right, so you want a fight, eh?
Snowball fight! Snowball fight!
One battle later —
Okay, okay! I surrender! So, listen — how come you didn't go on the holiday, then?
No cash! How about you, Mike?
I bust my leg playing rugby. It's almost mended, but the doc says no ski-ing. There are other winter sports, though! Let's take this crowd home and I'll fetch my sledge.
So, later —
GANGWAY!
Ha! Ha! Ha! This is brilliant!

Meanwhile, in France —
At last we're going ski-ing!
Lucky old Gemma. We're all stuck on the nursery slopes with Jonesy and SHE'S on the intermediate slopes with dishy Pierre!
Ooh! I'm w-wobbling!
Try to relax, Penny. Watch Arlene — she's got the hang of it. Good, Arlene!
Ouch!
At least you made it to the BOTTOM, Sita!
Later —
Tomorrow, you can move up to the intermediate slopes with Gemma, Arlene. You're quite good enough.
Lucky Arlene!
And, next day —
Excellent! I cannot believe that she has never before skied.
I knew Arlene would be good. She's dead sporty.

As the days passed, all the girls improved —
Whee!
Arlene loved every moment —
This is brill, Gemma!
AAAH!
Ow, my knee!
You have given it a very bad knock, Gemma. I think you had better stay off the skis now.
Poor old Gemma. We've only got another day to go, but the ski-ing's over for her.
Back at the chalet —
Hey, Arlene. We heard Pierre saying you were his most promising pupil of the week . . .
Naturally!
So we've got a prize for you . . .
FREE SNOWBALLS!
EEEK! You rotten lot!

Well, we're on our way home. Wonder how poor old Donna's been?
Fed-up, I'll bet. Look! I've bought her a present to cheer her up.
Back in Chesterford, they all met up at "Penny's Place" —
Donna! How are things?
Have you had a bad time?
Did Misery Miller make you work hard?
Fine, yes and no!
This is beautiful, Penny. Thanks! Listen, I'd love to hear all about your holiday, but, er — I've made a new friend, and I'm waiting for him right now!
HIM?
Hi, Donna! Ready?
You bet, Mike! See you! TOLD you I hadn't been having a bad time, girls!
Huh! And we've been feeling SORRY for her!
He's CUTE!
NEXT year, I think I'M staying behind!
Me, too! Ha! Ha! Ha!
THE END

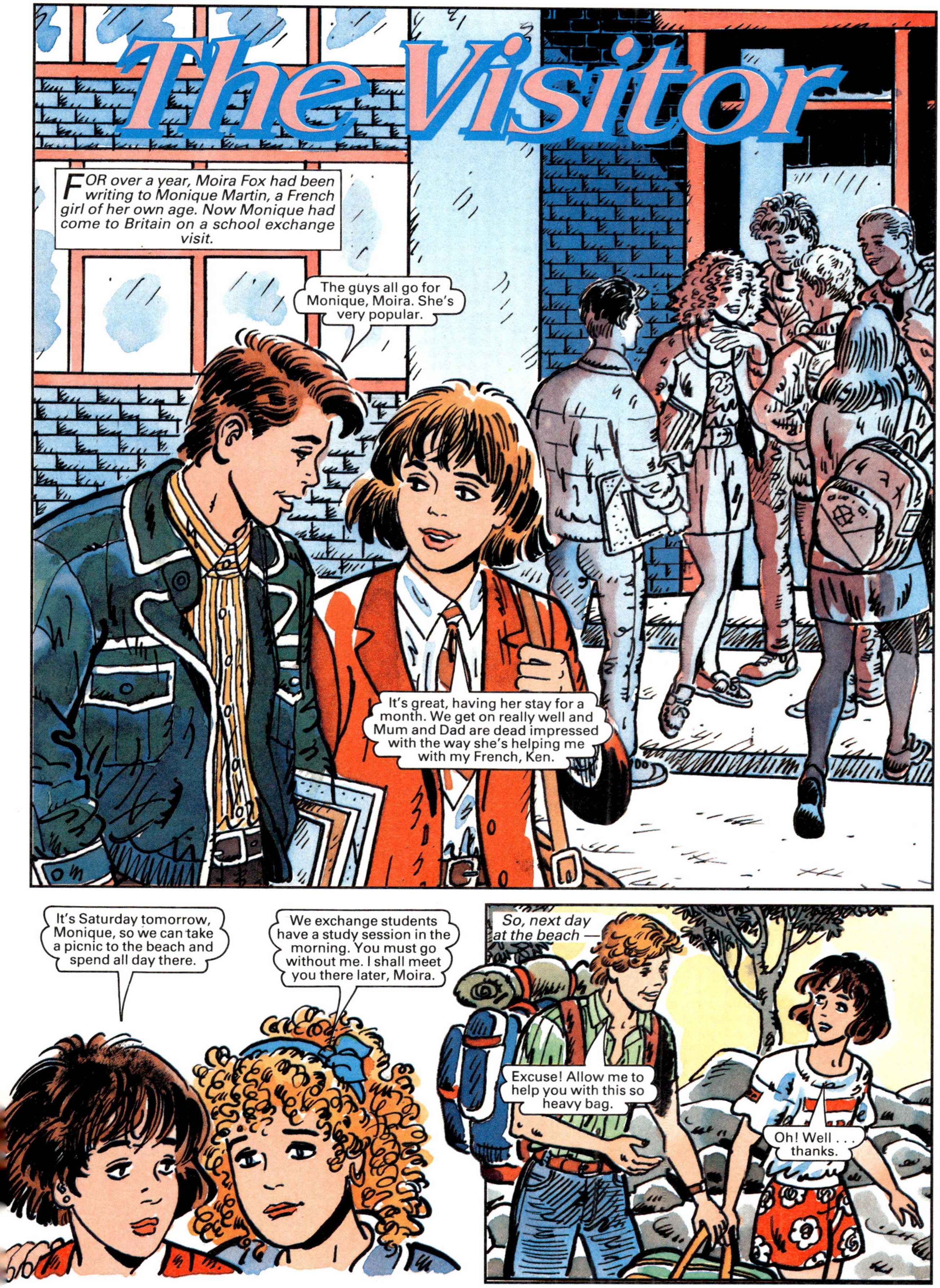
The Visitor
FOR over a year, Moira Fox had been writing to Monique Martin, a French girl of her own age. Now Monique had come to Britain on a school exchange visit.
The guys all go for Monique, Moira. She's very popular.
It's great, having her stay for a month. We get on really well and Mum and Dad are dead impressed with the way she's helping me with my French, Ken.
It's Saturday tomorrow, Monique, so we can take a picnic to the beach and spend all day there.
We exchange students have a study session in the morning. You must go without me. I shall meet you there later, Moira.
So, next day at the beach —
Excuse! Allow me to help you with this so heavy bag.
Oh! Well . . . thanks.

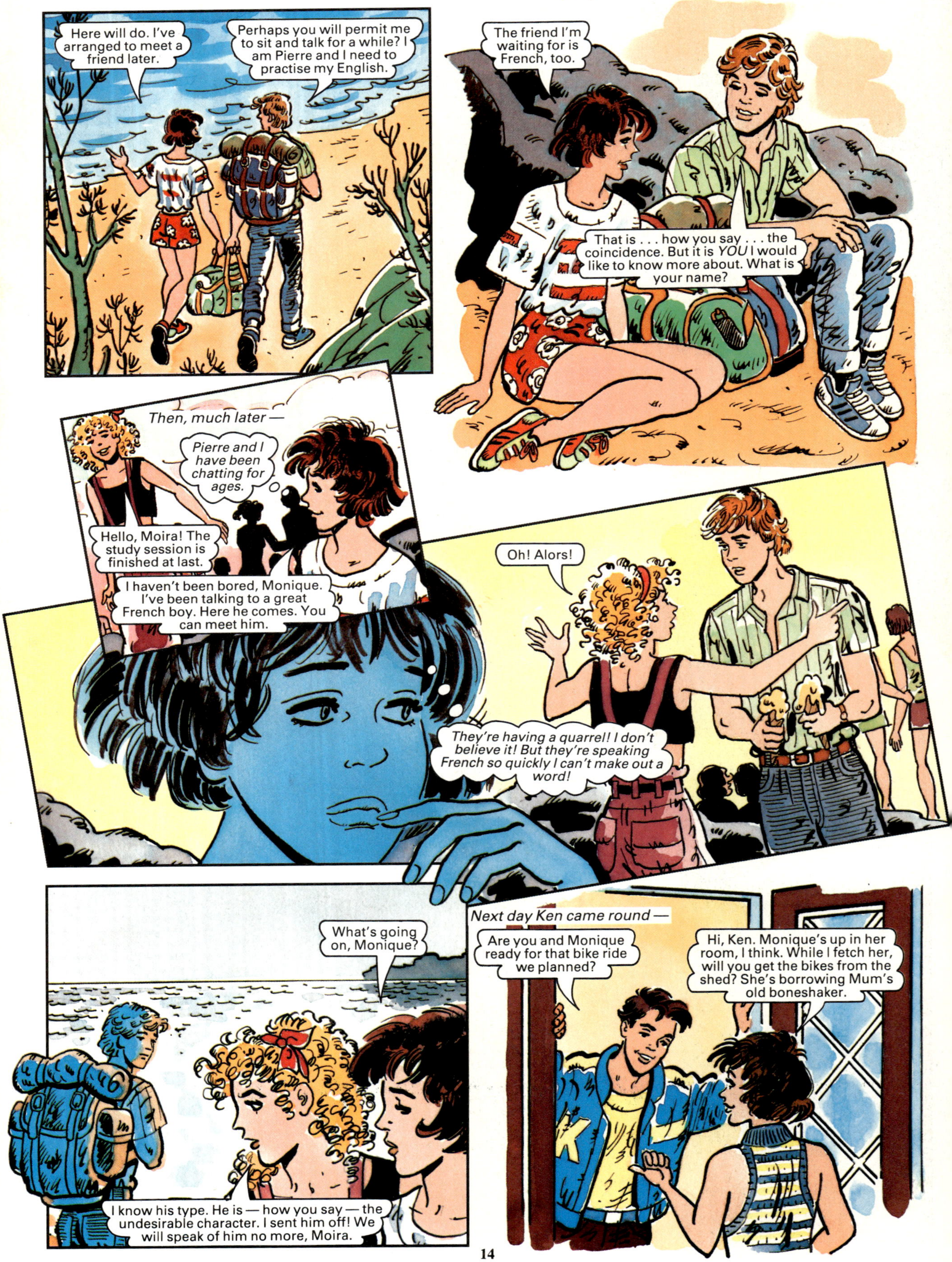
Here will do. I've arranged to meet a friend later.
Perhaps you will permit me to sit and talk for a while? I am Pierre and I need to practise my English.
The friend I'm waiting for is French, too.
That is . . . how you say . . . the coincidence. But it is YOU I would like to know more about. What is your name?
Then, much later —
Pierre and I have been chatting for ages.
Hello, Moira! The study session is finished at last.
I haven't been bored, Monique. I've been talking to a great French boy. Here he comes. You can meet him.
Oh! Alors!
They're having a quarrel! I don't believe it! But they're speaking French so quickly I can't make out a word!
What's going on, Monique?
I know his type. He is — how you say — the undesirable character. I sent him off! We will speak of him no more, Moira.
Next day Ken came round —
Are you and Monique ready for that bike ride we planned?
Hi, Ken. Monique's up in her room, I think. While I fetch her, will you get the bikes from the shed? She's borrowing Mum's old boneshaker.

But —
Hey, Ken! Monique doesn't seem to be around. I never heard her go out.
Wherever she is, I think she's gone on your mum's bike, because it's not here.
Then, in the kitchen —
Three packets of biscuits and some crisps have gone from here. WHO took them without asking?
Don't look at me, Mum! Maybe Dad's been raiding the pantry.
Later, Monique appeared —
I am sorry about our cycle ride. I went out alone and forgot the time, Moira. And now I have a headache and can't come out with you and Ken tonight.
Oh! Okay, then.
Then, that evening —
So much for Monique's headache! She was planning to meet a guy! Look! There she is in that café with him, Moira!
That's Pierre — the French boy I told you about! I don't reckon Monique's as nice as we thought. She sent him packing because he was chatting to ME — but then made a date to meet him HERSELF!
That night, Moira was awakened from an uneasy sleep —
I'm right! I was sure I heard Monique's door opening. Where's she going at two in the morning?
She's carrying something towards our shed. I must find out what's going on!

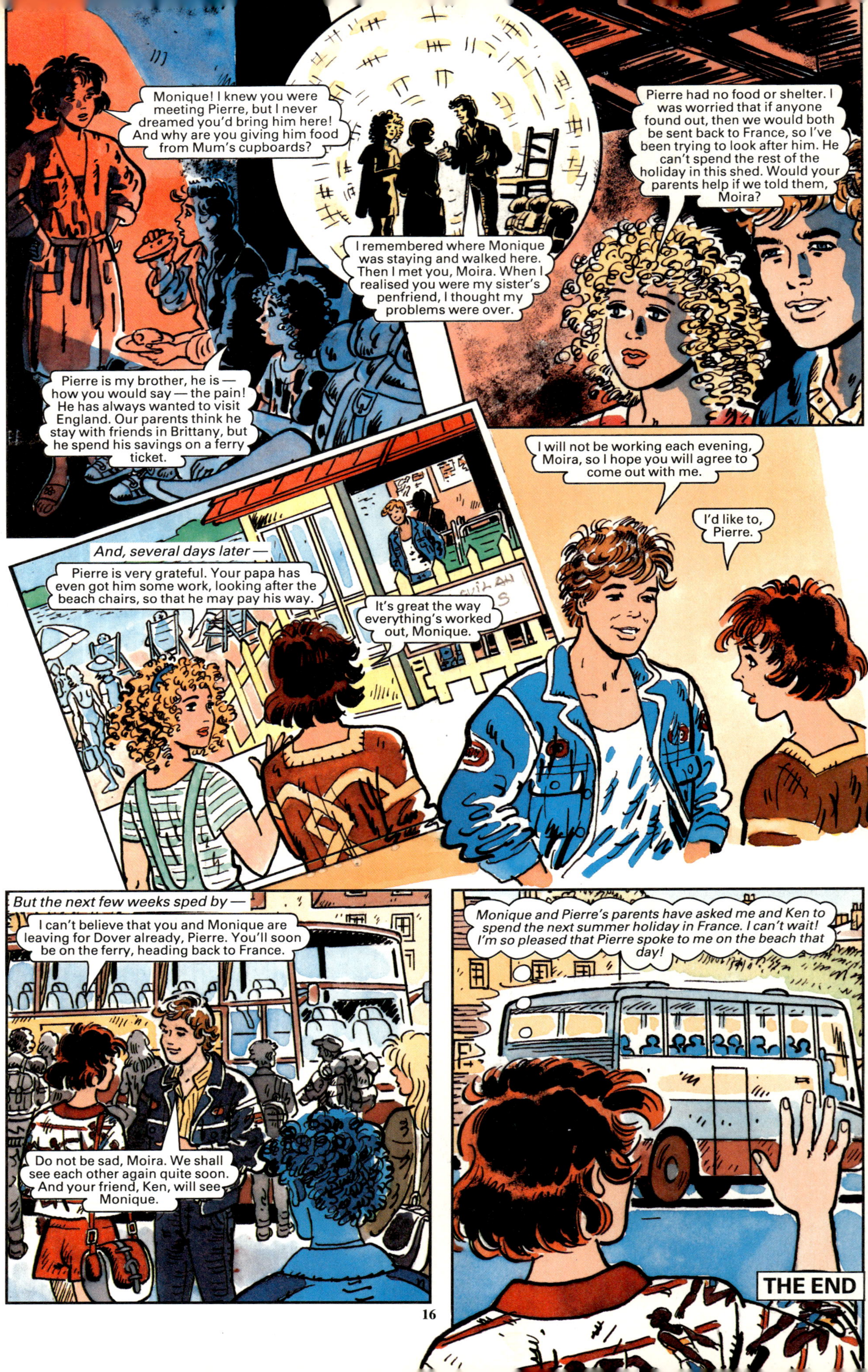
Monique! I knew you were meeting Pierre, but I never dreamed you'd bring him here! And why are you giving him food from Mum's cupboards?
Pierre is my brother, he is — how you would say — the pain! He has always wanted to visit England. Our parents think he stay with friends in Brittany, but he spend his savings on a ferry ticket.
I remembered where Monique was staying and walked here. Then I met you, Moira. When I realised you were my sister's penfriend, I thought my problems were over.
Pierre had no food or shelter. I was worried that if anyone found out, then we would both be sent back to France, so I've been trying to look after him. He can't spend the rest of the holiday in this shed. Would your parents help if we told them, Moira?
And, several days later —
Pierre is very grateful. Your papa has even got him some work, looking after the beach chairs, so that he may pay his way.
It's great the way everything's worked out, Monique.
I will not be working each evening, Moira, so I hope you will agree to come out with me.
I'd like to, Pierre.
But the next few weeks sped by —
I can't believe that you and Monique are leaving for Dover already, Pierre. You'll soon be on the ferry, heading back to France.
Do not be sad, Moira. We shall see each other again quite soon. And your friend, Ken, will see Monique.
Monique and Pierre's parents have asked me and Ken to spend the next summer holiday in France. I can't wait! I'm so pleased that Pierre spoke to me on the beach that day!
THE END

Memory

Our Jenny loved Memory very much! Every time I look at him I feel so sad! I can picture Jenny riding him.
I know what you mean. Oh! If only she hadn't gone on that holiday, and if the coach hadn't crashed . . .
MEMORY was a beautiful pony, but his owners, Mr and Mrs Gibson, were determined to sell him . . .

We'll have to make sure Memory goes to a good home. Jenny would have wanted that.
I'll advertise him in a specialist pony paper and we'll make sure that the people who buy him are nice.

So, a few weeks later—
He seems a friendly pony.
He is, Mr Brown. He's always pleased to see us when we come to his field.

We'd like to buy him. He's to be a surprise birthday present for our daughter, Julie. I'm sure she'll love him.
The Browns seem nice people. I feel happy about selling Memory to them.
A few days later—
Happy birthday, Julie.
Thanks, Mum and Dad! Is this my present?
A bridle! That's ace! I'll be able to use it when I ride Suzy at the stables.
No. This bridle isn't meant for Suzy. Come outside.
We thought it was time you had a pony of your own. Memory seemed perfect.
A PONY! Oh, thank you, Mum and Dad! He's gorgeous!
He stood perfectly still while you saddled him. He enjoys you tickling him behind his ear.
Yes!
But why did I do it? I've never done that to any of the riding school horses. I just suddenly seemed to sense he'd like it.

Soon—
You're heading for the downs, aren't you, boy? You must have guessed that's my favourite ride!
This is wonderful! Memory responds immediately to my every command. It's as if we've known each other for years and years.
Julie had previously been a good show jumper— but, riding Memory, her performance became inspired—
Clear round! That makes us class winners!
Success followed success. At last—
Good Luck, Julie.
The winner of this competition will qualify for the Junior Championship at the big horse show in London. It would be wonderful if Memory and I could get there.
It's a big course, but I know you won't let me down, Memory.

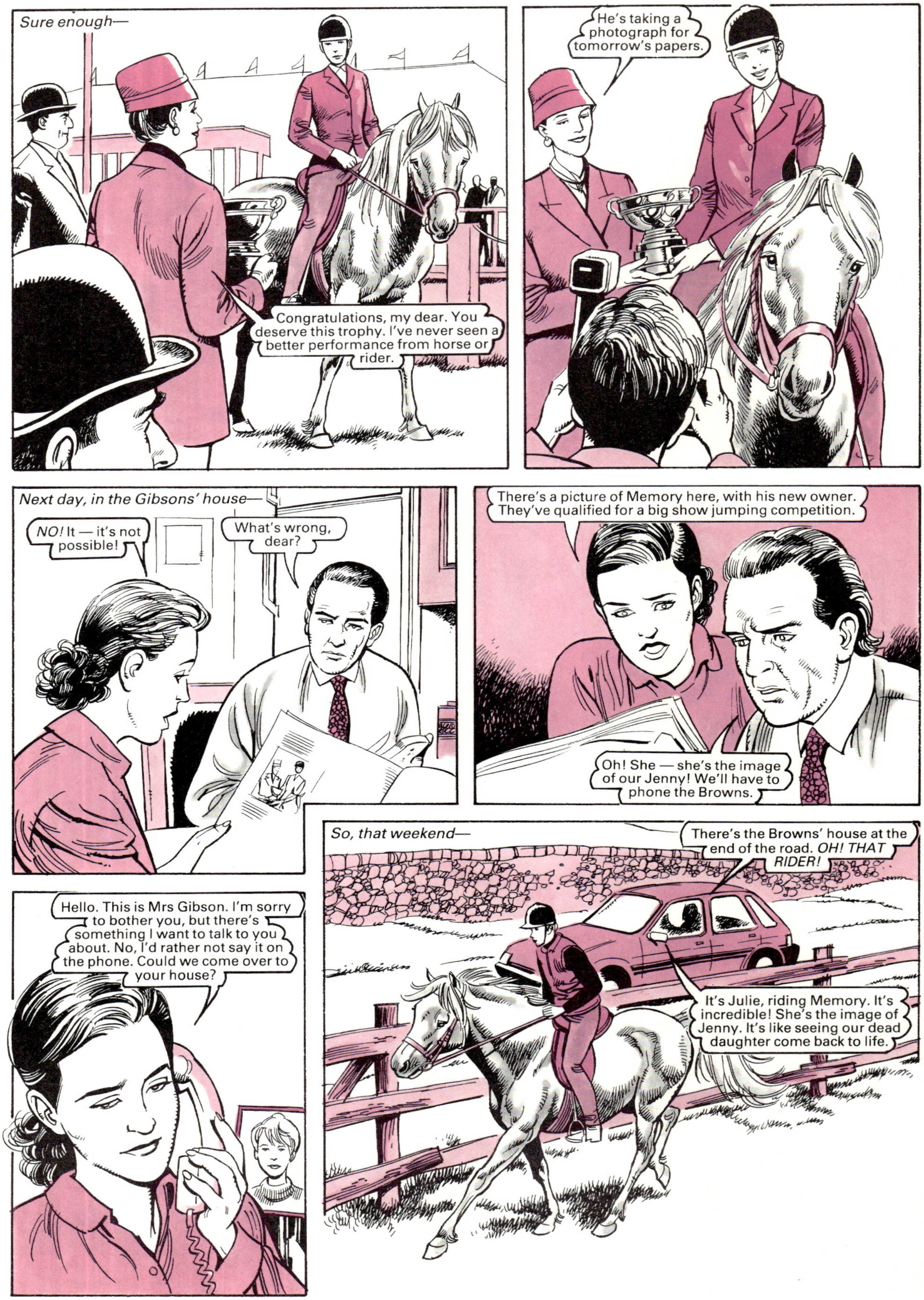
Sure enough—
Congratulations, my dear. You deserve this trophy. I've never seen a better performance from horse or rider.
He's taking a photograph for tomorrow's papers.
Next day, in the Gibsons' house—
NO! It — it's not possible!
What's wrong, dear?
There's a picture of Memory here, with his new owner. They've qualified for a big show jumping competition.
Oh! She — she's the image of our Jenny! We'll have to phone the Browns.
Hello. This is Mrs Gibson. I'm sorry to bother you, but there's something I want to talk to you about. No, I'd rather not say it on the phone. Could we come over to your house?
So, that weekend—
There's the Browns' house at the end of the road. OH! THAT RIDER!
It's Julie, riding Memory. It's incredible! She's the image of Jenny. It's like seeing our dead daughter come back to life.

At the house—
We were both stunned when we saw your daughter Julie's photograph. She's the image of OUR daughter, Jenny, who died.
Jenny was killed in a coach crash, you say? How DREADFUL!
We adopted Julie when she was just an infant. We can't imagine life without her.
We adopted JENNY, too! Look! Here's a photo of her, taken last year.
Oh! I see what you mean. She looks EXACTLY the same as our Julie. I think we should compare adoption papers.
Soon, they realised the truth—
You and Jenny were sisters, Julie. She was your twin.
I never realised I had a sister. I'm so sad I never knew her.
But knowing I own her horse makes me feel close to Jenny. Maybe that explains the instant bond there was between Memory and me.
And there's SOMETHING I can do for her. I'll win the Junior Championship on Memory in honour of her!
What a kind thought!
You must come with us to see Julie compete.

So, on the big day—
Good luck, Julie! I hope Memory goes well for you.
I'd like you to have something else of Jenny's, as well as her horse . . .
We bought this brand new riding outfit for Jenny to wear in her next competition. Sadly she died before it took place.
Thank you, Mrs Gibson.
It fits perfectly.
Are you ready, Memory?
And the next competitor is Julie Brown on Memory.
Here we go!
I'm doing this for you, Jenny. All for you!
Julie and Memory jumped magnificently—
And it looks like an unbeatable time for Julie Brown in this jump off!
It — it could almost be Jenny out there! I feel so proud.

And—
Congratulations, darling! You won!
Thank you for achieving that for Jenny. And thank YOU Mr and Mrs Brown, for letting us share in Julie's big day.
I hope you'll share other days with us, too. Keep in touch. We'd like you to become a sort of aunt and uncle to Julie.
Thank you. We'd like that. Somehow, losing Jenny doesn't seem quite so bad now we've found Julie.
A few days later—
This is my first visit to Jenny's home. But, before I go to the house, there's someone else I want to visit first . . .
This is the place. I want to give my winner's sash and rosette to Jenny.
For you, Jenny. With all my love — from your sister . . . the sister you never knew.
JENNY GIBSON
1980-1994
THE END

Holiday Magic

Later—
Have you got Mark's address and phone number, Nicola?
No, Liz. We had a great time, but we know what we felt was just holiday magic. It will fade with the tan!
But Nicola found she couldn't forget Mark—
Rats, it's freezing, Nicola. I HATE February! You're quiet. What's wrong?
I was just thinking about someone, Suzy.
I was thinking about Mark. I can't forget him.
See you tomorrow.
Yeah. 'Bye, Suzy.
It's six months since I've seen Mark, but I haven't met anyone I like even half as much!
When Nicola got home—
I've got some holiday brochures, Liz. They're the best cure I know for winter blues!
Ooh, let's see that one, Mum!
SUNNDAY HOLIDAYS
How about canoeing?
Get lost! I once went with the school. It's mega-boring!
I agree, Liz. I want to have a relaxing holiday, Paul.

What do YOU think, Nicola?
I'm not bothered, Mum.
Wherever we go won't be a patch on last year — not without Mark.
Have a look at this one and see if there's anything you fancy.
This picture of a quiet beach reminds me of that last day with Mark. I miss him! And that figure right down by the shore . . .
SUNNYDAY TOURS
. . . it looks a bit like Mark. Oh, I wish we'd kept in touch!
SUNNYDAY TOURS
Next day, Nicola was still unhappy—
Stapleham, where he lives, is about forty miles from here. That's a long way, but we could have met sometimes.
Letter for you, Nicola!
SHREDS

It — it has a Stapleham postmark! Could it be?
Hey! Where are you going, Nicola?
It must be from Mark! I'll read it in my room!
The guy you met last year on holiday? But you said you didn't give him your address, so how come he's written to you?
It IS from Mark! He says he remembered part of my address from a competition entry I filled in when we were together and he got the rest from the phone directories in his local library.
...so maybe you won't be pleased to hear from me, but let me know, because I've missed you. I've wanted to write for ages, in spite of what we said...
Nicola wrote back to Mark and, the following Saturday—
MARK!
Hi, Nicola! I hope you didn't mind me writing.
I'm sure some people do find that a holiday romance was just holiday magic — but I like you here, in winter, just as much as in Devon in summer!
I feel like that about you, Mark.

Two weeks later in Mark's town—
When you wrote, you said your family are going to Wales on holiday this year, in July. So are mine — to the SAME place!
It's with SUNNYDAY TOURS. I'm pleased about that, because I finally decided to write to you when Dad brought the holiday brochure home.
The current Sunnyday one had a picture of a deserted beach on the cover — well, deserted except for one figure, which I thought looked like you, and made me want to see you.
That's odd, Mark.
I saw someone who looked like YOU on the cover of a brochure, too!
When Nicola got home—
This is weird! This IS the same brochure — but now there seem to be TWO figures — Mark AND me!
SUNNYDAY TOURS
Maybe you can still get a little holiday magic even when you're NOT on holiday!
THE END

A FRIEND for KEEPS

Then, one day —
What's the matter, Tara?
My best friend's moved away. I'm going to be really lonely on my own, Katie.
Like me!
I'm sorry, Katie. I never realised how left out you must feel. Hey! Why don't *WE* pal up?
Soon —
Tara, there's a school disco tonight. Fancy going?
You bet!
It's cosmic having Tara for a friend.
The girls often walked Tara's dog, Blue —
Good girl, Blue! *FETCH!*
One day —
Great news! Blue's expecting puppies!
That's excellent!

They're due in about a month.
Blue's a lovely dog. I'm sure her puppies will be lovely, too.
At last —
Four pups, Katie! They were born last night.
They're beautiful, Tara!
Oh, Blue! You *ARE* a clever girl!
I'm so happy! I wish I could stay here with Tara and Blue for ever, but I know that can't happen.
Sure enough, a few weeks later —
The manager called me in today. They're moving me to the Porthampton branch.
Porthampton? But that's *MILES* away, Dad!
I won't go! I want to stay here.
Don't be silly, Katie! You can't stay. Dad has to go where his work takes him — and we go with Dad. I'll find out about accommodation in Porthampton tomorrow.
Before long —
So you leave on Saturday. I'm as fed up about it as you are, Katie. I'll miss you. I suppose we'll both have to make new friends.
Yes. But at least when you pal up with someone new, you'll know you and her can stay together I *NEVER* have a friend for keeps!

You will *THIS* time, Katie!
Who?
One of Blue's puppies! I chose Sheba because she looks most like Blue. She's old enough to leave Blue now, and I want you to have her, Katie!
I've cleared it with your parents. They thought it was a great idea. Sheba's all yours!
Oh, thank you, Tara.
Saturday came —
Goodbye, Tara! I'll write!
We can exchange news about the dogs!
ROBINSONS REMOVALS
I'm still sad about moving, but at least now — even if I can't ever be with my human friends for more than a few months — I have Sheba, who'll stay with me. A friend for keeps!
THE END

THREE CHEERS FOR MANDY m&J JUDY

FULL OF YOUR FAVE GOODIES!

Kate Bulger, Croydon

Sarah Martin, Whitehead

Jo Cooper, Dunstable

Clare Louise Chiappe, Gibraltar

Dawn Naylor, Nottingham

ALL THESE READERS CAN'T BE WRONG!

Felicity Milner, Northallerton

Sian Douglas, Essex

Make sure you don't miss out anything important — this handy calendar will keep you right.

JANUARY

S	1	8	15	22	29
M	2	9	16	23	30
Tu	3	10	17	24	31
W	4	11	18	25	—
Th	5	12	19	26	—
F	6	13	20	27	—
S	7	14	21	28	—

IMPORTANT DATES

FEBRUARY

S	—	5	12	19	26
M	—	6	13	20	27
Tu	—	7	14	21	28
W	1	8	15	22	—
Th	2	9	16	23	—
F	3	10	17	24	—
S	4	11	18	25	—

MARCH

S	—	5	12	19	26
M	—	6	13	20	27
Tu	—	7	14	21	28
W	1	8	15	22	29
Th	2	9	16	23	30
F	3	10	17	24	31
S	4	11	18	25	—

APRIL

S	—	2	9	16	23/30
M	—	3	10	17	24
Tu	—	4	11	18	25
W	—	5	12	19	26
Th	—	6	13	20	27
F	—	7	14	21	28
S	1	8	15	22	29

CHEEPY 'N' CREEPY!

Life At LONDON ZOO

We know that you all lurve animals, but Amanda Ferguson is daft about them. She's lucky enough to work as a keeper at London Zoo. Amanda had a lot of pets when she was young and knew she wanted a job working with animals, so she studied Animal Science after leaving school. Then she worked in riding-stables and a laboratory and eventually started as a trainee bird keeper at London Zoo, 5 years ago. We had a birrova chinwag with Amanda and she told us all about her fabsy job.

Time for a stroll.

What's goin' on in here, then?

LONDON ZOO

CONSERVATION IN ACTION

"At first, you have to do all the mucky jobs. There is somebody watching and teaching you all the time, until you are ready to look after the animals by yourself. You start with ones that are not very dangerous or valuable. I had to feed the birds, clean out their enclosures and watch carefully to see that they stayed healthy.

Some birds, like ducks, don't recognise the keepers at all, although they get excited when they see our brown uniforms, because they know it might be dinner-time! Other birds, such as the parrots, get to know us quite well. My faves are the penguins because you learn to tell them apart and they all have different personalities.

An important part of our job is telling visitors about the animals and why we are keeping them in captivity. We keep black-footed penguins here. They come from South Africa and although there are still a lot of them, they may soon be threatened with extinction. Their numbers are falling rapidly because of oil pollution and overfishing, as well as building on the coast where they breed. Pairs nest in burrows and take turns to sit on their eggs. Here at London Zoo, they make nests in special boxes around their pool. The other penguins are dead nosy and they all try to see inside, but they are unwelcome guests and are chased away. It gets very noisy!

After an egg hatches, we put the chick in an incubator and rear it by hand, in case it gets too wet by the pool. Chicks are fed with mashed fish which is really, really smelly. Sometimes, we have to come back at night to feed a baby, but it's all worth it when we see them grow.

My job is brilliant and I love it, but it does get very cold and wet working outside in the winter and in summer we have to work long hours."

Amanda recently had a short break from the cold, when she went to work at London Zoo's Invertebrate House.

This is where the insects and snails are kept. Because birds eat these creatures, Amanda wanted to learn more about them. She also wanted to find out how endangered animals, like bird-eating spiders, are bred at London Zoo. Yuk — bird-eating spiders! Sounds a bit creepy to us!

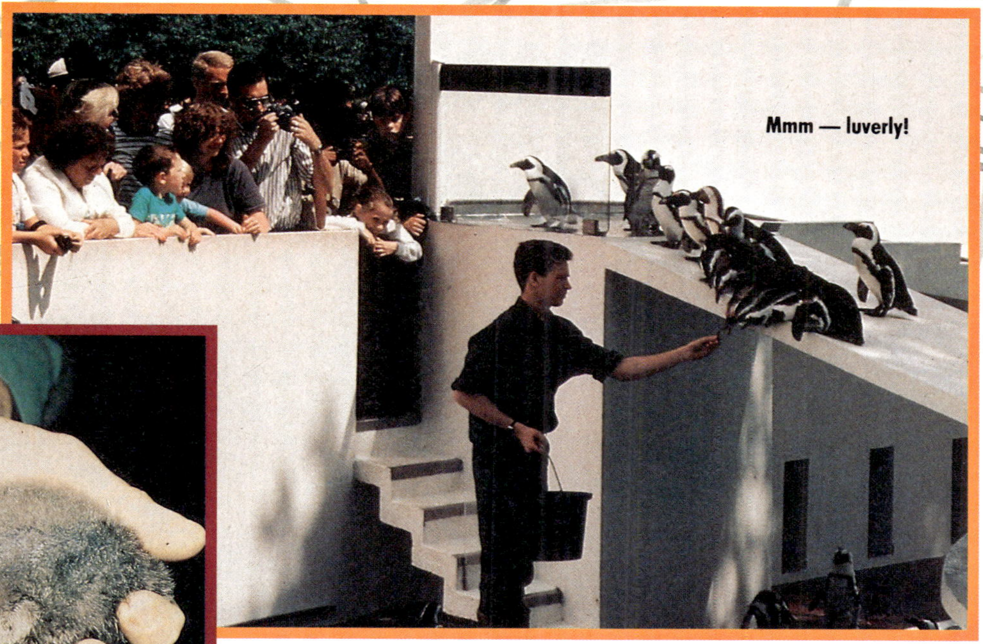

Mmm — luverly!

Awww!

I'm coming to get you!

He's harmless — honest!

SIMPLY THE Best

Not sure what type of boy suits you? Well, check out our fun quiz to find your ideal match.

1. If you were being whisked off on your dream date what would it be?
(a) Off to the cinema to see a funny film with plenty of sweets to eat and popcorn to flick.
(b) Something active like skating or a game of table tennis at the Youth Club.
(c) A nice stroll in the park and then maybe a burger or a coffee.
(d) Nothing less than being taken to a very posh restaurant for a slap-up meal, given flowers and generally being spoiled rotten.

2. Out of these famous peeps who would you most like to be?
(d) Madonna
(a) Whoopi Goldberg
(c) Saffron from 'Absolutely Fabulous'
(b) Anthea Turner

3. What's your fave type of music?
(c) You hate anything that's too loud, but Take That aren't bad.
(d) Dance music — you love to get boogying at the disco, showing off your latest routines.
(a) Most pop stuff that you can sing along to, but you're not too keen on the slushy songs.
(b) You like dance music, too. All that dancing helps keep you fit.

4. What's your dream holiday destination?
(b) Surfing, scuba diving and water skiing in Australia.
(d) Hollywood — mingling with all the stars.
(c) Your own desert island where you can get loadsa peace 'n' quiet.
(a) Fun-filled Florida — Disney World, theme parks, sunshine and lots to do.

5. Pick your fave colour.
(c) Pink
(d) Red
(a) Yellow
(b) Green.

6. Which of these TV progs do you really hate to miss?
(a) Roseanne, The Big Breakfast.
(c) Corrie, Brookie and EastEnders.
(b) Athletics, Grandstand, the Olympics.
(d) Mini series, film premieres and the Oscars.

7. When you go to the hairdresser's how do you have your hair done?
(c) Usually just a trim — you're not sure about trying out new styles.
(d) You like to look glam and you have the stylist twist your long locks into a truly sophisticated style.
(a) You lurve to try something different every time you go.
(b) Something short 'n' neat. You don't have time to mess about with gels and sprays.

8. Santa brings you new P.J.s. What are they like?
(b) They're stretchy with a baggy t-shirt top and short bottoms.
(d) Glamorous, satin, film star type ones.
(c) A cosy, cuddly sleepsuit and matching robe. Oh, and don't forget the fluffy slippers — you've got to be warm.
(a) A bright night shirt with a wacky cartoon character pic on the front.

CONCLUSIONS

MOSTLY A'S

You're a cheery little person aren't you? You love having a laugh and you're always on the go. Bright colours are your faves and your mates are really important to you. When you go out with a boy you aim to enjoy yourself and don't get too uptight about it. If it doesn't work out it doesn't matter cos you've got plenty of time for serious lurve things when you're older.

Your Dream Date would be someone like Dan Falzon. He's a bright, boy-next-door type, but also a birrova joker. Life wouldn't be dull with him around.

MOSTLY B'S

You're no couch potato! You love sport and exercise and can't wait to get out 'n' about. There's not really much time left for boys, but the ones that you do like have got to share your hobbies.

A Dream Date for you would be going out for a jog with Scott Michaelson. This handsome chap obviously lurves sport as much as you do — and you'd have no bother getting outta bed at the crack of dawn to go surfin' with him.

MOSTLY C'S

What a quiet little mouse you are. You like to spend time on your own and you're not really that interested in boys. You're also quite shy and a bit unsure where they're concerned. Fashion and clothes aren't too important with you either, so although you like to look smart and neat, your outfits aren't super trendy.

Mark Owen from Take That would be your Dream Date. Although he's gorgeous and in a top pop group, we know he's a sensitive little soul at heart. You'd have no probs getting him to do all the rowing when you have a go on the boats in the park.

MOSTLY D'S

Wow! You like to be noticed at ALL times. Always in the latest gear and always lookin' your very best. You want to be a STAR! It's a major disaster if you have a hair out of place and you certainly couldn't be seen with a guy who is anything less than drop dead gorgeous. When you meet someone you like you're totally lurve struck — for about two weeks until you meet somebody better, that is.

Your Dream Date's just gotta be Superman — who else? He's handsome, he's hunky and he could whisk you off to all those faraway places you dream of in the blink of an eye. Have a nice time!

PUZZLES 'N' THINGS

This year we've got 12 pages of extra-fab puzzles to put your brainbox to the test. So, get busy, girlies — NOW!

POP SQUARE

Below you'll find lists of pop stars and groups. They can all be found in straight lines in any direction: up, down, backwards, forwards or diagonally. Letters may be used more than once.

ALISON LIMERICK
APACHE INDIAN
BAD BOYS INC
BJORK
BON JOVI
BRYAN ADAMS
CULTURE BEAT
DANNII
ETERNAL
EXTREME
GABRIELLE
INXS
INNER CIRCLE
JANET JACKSON
JAMIROQUAI
JASON DONOVAN
JOEY LAWRENCE
KIM APPLEBY
MADONNA
MEATLOAF
M PEOPLE
NEW ORDER
PRINCE
SHAGGY

A	C	U	L	T	U	R	E	B	E	A	T	E	J	J	I
L	P	B	M	E	A	T	L	O	A	F	A	C	A	A	N
I	K	A	A	B	E	L	P	O	E	P	M	N	S	N	N
S	I	D	C	N	E	W	O	R	D	E	R	E	O	E	E
O	M	B	C	H	G	F	P	A	B	S	B	R	N	T	R
N	A	O	D	H	E	S	R	C	E	M	C	W	D	J	C
L	P	Y	J	E	X	I	I	D	L	A	D	A	O	A	I
I	P	S	K	N	T	Y	N	E	L	D	E	L	N	C	R
M	L	I	I	L	R	G	C	D	E	A	A	Y	O	S	C
E	E	N	M	B	E	G	E	F	I	N	P	E	V	O	L
R	B	C	J	O	M	A	F	G	R	A	R	O	A	N	E
I	Y	O	N	N	E	H	G	E	B	Y	N	J	N	H	X
C	R	P	O	J	A	S	T	H	A	R	S	S	R	O	J
K	R	S	O	O	L	E	J	K	G	B	T	T	V	W	K
W	V	T	N	V	M	I	A	U	Q	O	R	I	M	A	J
D	A	N	N	I	I	M	A	D	O	N	N	A	N	M	L

TRIVIA PUZZLES

Time to test those brain cells with these easy-peasy trivia questions. Each set of five questions on different subjects can be answered in under 60 seconds. Go for it — NOW!

SPORTS

1. What sport has the same name as an orange drink?
2. Which sport is played at Wimbledon?
3. For which sport is Frank Bruno famous?
4. Which sport used to be called ping-pong?
5. Which sport has line-outs?

NUMBERS

1. What number is said to be unlucky?
2. How many people are there in a soccer team?
3. How many signs of the Zodiac are there?
4. How many Walt Disney dalmatians are there?
5. How many dates do Blind Date contestants have to choose from?

PLACES

1. Where did Mark Owen go to school?
2. What is the nearest country to the Isle of Wight?
3. Which Italian city is famous for its canals?
4. What foreign country is nearest to London?
5. Which Lancashire seaside town has a famous tower?

ANIMALS

1. What kind of animal is a collie?
2. What kind of animal was Black Beauty?
3. What kind of animal is Garfield?
4. What kind of animal is Mrs Tiggywinkle?
5. Name the animal that resembles a crossing.

CARTOONS

1. Which little fawn had a rabbit friend called Thumper?
2. Who owns Snoopy?
3. What Beano character is a Lord?
4. What is the name of the boy in The Jungle Book?
5. What is Desperate Dan's favourite food?

COLOURS

1. What colour is produced by mixing yellow and blue?
2. What colour are Smurfs?
3. What are the two main colours of Pepsi and Coca Cola cans?
4. What two colours are magpies?
5. What colour was the itsy bitsy polka dot bikini with which Timmy Mallett had a hit?

Trivial Pursuit

Trivial Pursuit is a registered trademark of Horn Abbot International Ltd.

ANSWERS ON PAGE 112

HA!HA!

Mother: Why did you put this frog in your brother's bed?
Girl: I couldn't find a dead mouse!

What's red and flickers?
An apple with a loose connection!

What do you get after it's been taken?
Your photograph!

Mummy, Mummy! I've got Daddy's ladder.
What did Daddy say?
AAAAAGGGHH!

How do you keep an 'M&J' reader in suspense?
We're not going to tell you!

What do you get if you cross a penguin with a lamb?
A sheepskin dinner jacket!

Why was the lion-tamer towed away?
He parked on a yellow lion!

What do you call a sick crocodile?
An illigator!

Why are sardines stupid?
They get into tins and leave the key outside!

Waiter! This water is cloudy.
No it's not, the glass is dirty, Sir!

Why did the policeman wear purple braces?
To keep his trousers up!

Which animal should you take on a day out in the country?
A picnic hamster!

What kind of plate does a skeleton eat from?
Bone China!

What do you call a Scotsman who serves school dinners?
Dinner Ken!

Why didn't the skeleton go to the dance?
Because he had no body to go with!

Why is fog like a lost boy?
They are both mist (missed)!

What do you call a boy with a shovel on his head?
Doug!

What sits in a pram and wobbles?
A jelly baby!

Where do parrots learn to talk?
At a polytechnic!

TAKE THAT quiz

Think you're a big TAKE THAT fan, do you? Get stuck into this quiz and we'll soon find out who the REAL fans are!

1. Which member of the band was a painter for over three years?
2. Which year was Jason born? 1970, 1969, 1968?
3. What is Howard's middle name?
4. Which member of the band is the youngest?
5. Where was Mark born?
6. Which member of the band played Joseph in Joseph And The Amazing Technicolour Dreamcoat at school?
7. Which member of the group kept an iguana called Nirvana?
8. Which member of the band is a twin?
9. What was Robbie's first job after leaving school?
10. What is Mark's nickname? Batty, Booter or Bingo?
11. What was the band's first single?
12. Take That used to have another name. What was it?
13. Which member of the band is a Port Vale supporter?
14. What was the band's first Top Twenty hit?
15. What is Mark's brother's name?
16. Robbie once played the Artful Dodger. True or False?
17. What album did the band bring out in August 1992?
18. Complete this song title. Could It Be -----.

ANSWERS

1. Jason; 2. 1970; 3. Paul; 4. Robbie; 5. Oldham; 6. Gary; 7. Mark; 8. Jason; 9. Robbie was a double-glazing salesman; 10. Booter; 11. Do What U Like; 12. Take That And Party; 13. Robbie; 14. It Only Takes A Minute; 15. Daniel; 16. True; 17. Take That And Party; 18. Magic.

SCORES

0-6 Naughty, naughty! You're spending too much time gazin' at the lads and not enough reading about them.

6-12 Pretty good! You obviously know quite a bit about TAKE THAT. Just a little bit more studying required. However, I'm sure you won't mind.

12-18 You're either TAKE THAT'S No. 1 fan or else you cheated and looked at the answers. Come on, tell the truth . . .

MINI SQUARES

There are three mini wordsquares below. Words may be read forwards, backwards, up, down or diagonally. Letters may be used more than once.

Wildlife

D	R	A	P	O	E	L	B	A
B	T	F	L	L	G	E	U	A
L	E	I	L	H	R	L	F	L
D	O	A	G	A	Z	E	F	L
N	M	K	G	E	E	P	A	I
A	J	U	B	P	R	H	L	R
I	O	R	L	R	T	A	O	O
C	A	M	N	S	A	N	B	G
O	K	O	A	L	A	T	C	D

TIGER
LION
ELEPHANT
ZEBRA
GORILLA
LEOPARD
BUFFALO
COUGAR
LLAMA
KOALA

Birds

C	E	A	W	X	Y	B	G	A
D	A	N	A	W	S	L	T	H
T	G	N	H	O	F	A	N	A
O	L	B	A	R	Z	C	A	J
R	E	C	W	R	E	K	S	B
R	P	R	K	A	Y	B	A	N
A	C	O	L	P	K	I	E	E
P	O	W	V	S	L	R	H	R
M	N	F	T	S	E	D	P	W

CANARY
EAGLE
BLACKBIRD
SPARROW
HAWK
SWAN
CROW
WREN
PARROT
PHEASANT

Sports

TENNIS
SWIMMING
SQUASH
NETBALL
HOCKEY
RUGBY
CRICKET
GOLF
POLO
SKIING

S	F	G	D	C	A	P	S	E
Q	W	P	O	L	O	I	F	H
U	C	I	H	A	N	B	O	G
A	R	J	M	N	K	C	N	R
S	I	K	E	M	K	I	G	U
H	C	T	L	E	I	T	J	G
N	K	M	Y	K	S	N	H	B
O	E	R	S	F	L	O	G	Y
P	T	N	E	T	B	A	L	L

CROSSWORDS

Across:

1. Golden-yellow flower (9)
5. Break (4)
7. Store (4)
8. Blast of a horn (4)
10. Cabbage centre (5)
13. Tells lies (4)
14. Journey (4)
15. Bed cover (9)

Down:

1. Lie in the sun (4)
2. Take this group (4)
3. Incision (3)
4. Animal's feet (4)
6. Card game (5)
7. Commence (5)
9. Hint (4)
10. Deal of cards (4)
11. Threesome (4)
12. Outer covering (4)

Across:

3. Boundary (5)
5. Tend (5)
6. Female relative (5)
8. Best (6)
12. Easy (6)
15. Clear liquid (5)
16. Large sea (5)
17. Yellow fruit (5)

ANSWERS ON PAGE 112

Down:

1. Item of cutlery (5)
2. Small bird (4)
3. Camera part (4)
4. Bad Boys --- (3)
7. Piece of news (4)
9. Relieve (4)
10. Vegetables (5)
11. Piece of luggage (4)
13. Hard metal (4)
14. Victim (4)

MORE PUZZLES 'N' THINGS ON PAGE 87

MAY					
S	—	7	14	21	28
M	1	8	15	22	29
Tu	2	9	16	23	30
W	3	10	17	24	31
Th	4	11	18	25	—
F	5	12	19	26	—
S	6	13	20	27	—

JUNE					
S	—	4	11	18	25
M	—	5	12	19	26
Tu	—	6	13	20	27
W	—	7	14	21	28
Th	1	8	15	22	29
F	2	9	16	23	30
S	3	10	17	24	—

JULY					
S	—	2	9	16	23/30
M	—	3	10	17	24/31
Tu	—	4	11	18	25
W	—	5	12	19	26
Th	—	6	13	20	27
F	—	7	14	21	28
S	1	8	15	22	29

AUGUST

S	—	6	13	20	27
M	—	7	14	21	28
Tu	1	8	15	22	29
W	2	9	16	23	30
Th	3	10	17	24	31
F	4	11	18	25	—
S	5	12	19	26	—

IMPORTANT DATES

make 'n' do

Hi there, peeps! Fiona here. There's always loadsa rubbish left over from Christmas, isn't there? Well, I know all you girlies like to be green, so I've got loadsa ideas for recycling all the used stuff into many fabsy things. Have fun!

BOTTLED UP

You'll need:- Empty glass bottles (we used ones that had had foam bath in them); gold or silver craft paint; thin gold or silver cord; craft glue; stick on jewels; sequins (you can buy a metre of assorted colours on a string for around 40p); corks.

What to do:

Making these posho bottles couldn't be easier and you can use them for storing sweets, saving money (5p's add up quickly) or refill them with cheaper bath foam.

First paint the cork for each bottle with the craft paint and leave to dry. Next, put a little blob of glue on the the end of the cord, stick it to the neck of the bottle and carefully start to wind it round. When the neck is covered, cut off any extra cord and secure the loose end with another touch of glue. If your corks are dry, you can now decorate them. We stuck a jewel to the top and glued sequins round the top edge. You can also decorate the glass with sequins and jewels if you like. And that's it — easy, eh?

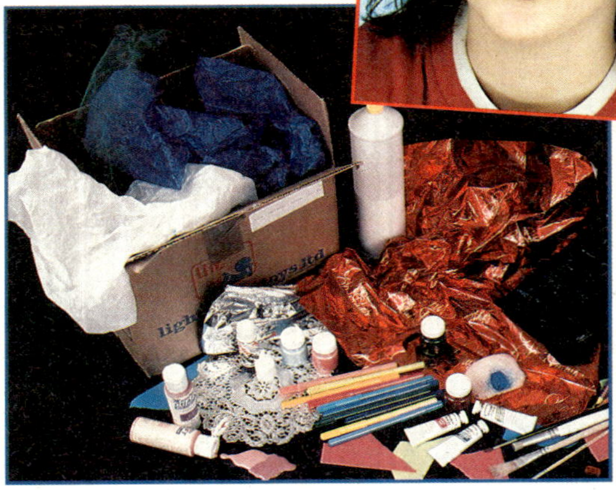

MIRROR MAGIC

You'll need:- Left over paper plates; scraps of old tissue paper; bits of string; PVA (school) glue; paint or nail polish; a small handbag mirror.

What to do:

If your paper plates are quite thin, stick two together to make a firm base. Leave to dry out. Now choose the design you'd like and mark it out on the plate. Stick the bits of string round your design — this will give the mirror frame a raised, 3-D effect. Mix some glue with a little water so that it's thin enough to paint on and rip your tissue up into little bits. Now paint a small part of the plate with the glue and stick down the tissue. Overlap the edges as you go so that no white shines through and press the tissue carefully round the string. Make sure the glue soaks right through the tissue — don't worry, PVA glue dries clear. You may need to put on two layers of tissue, but let the first one dry out before starting again. When you come to the edges of the plate, just let the tissue hang over — you can trim it with scissors when it's dry. When you've put on all the tissue, paint over the whole plate with glue and leave to dry thoroughly.

Now your plate should be nice and hard. All you gotta do to finish it is pick out the string design with some contrasting paint and stick on the mirror (ours cost 69p from Superdrug). If you don't want to make a mirror, just make lots of differently designed plates to decorate your room.

Check out pages 84 & 85 for more groovy recycling ideas.

STAGE SCHOOL

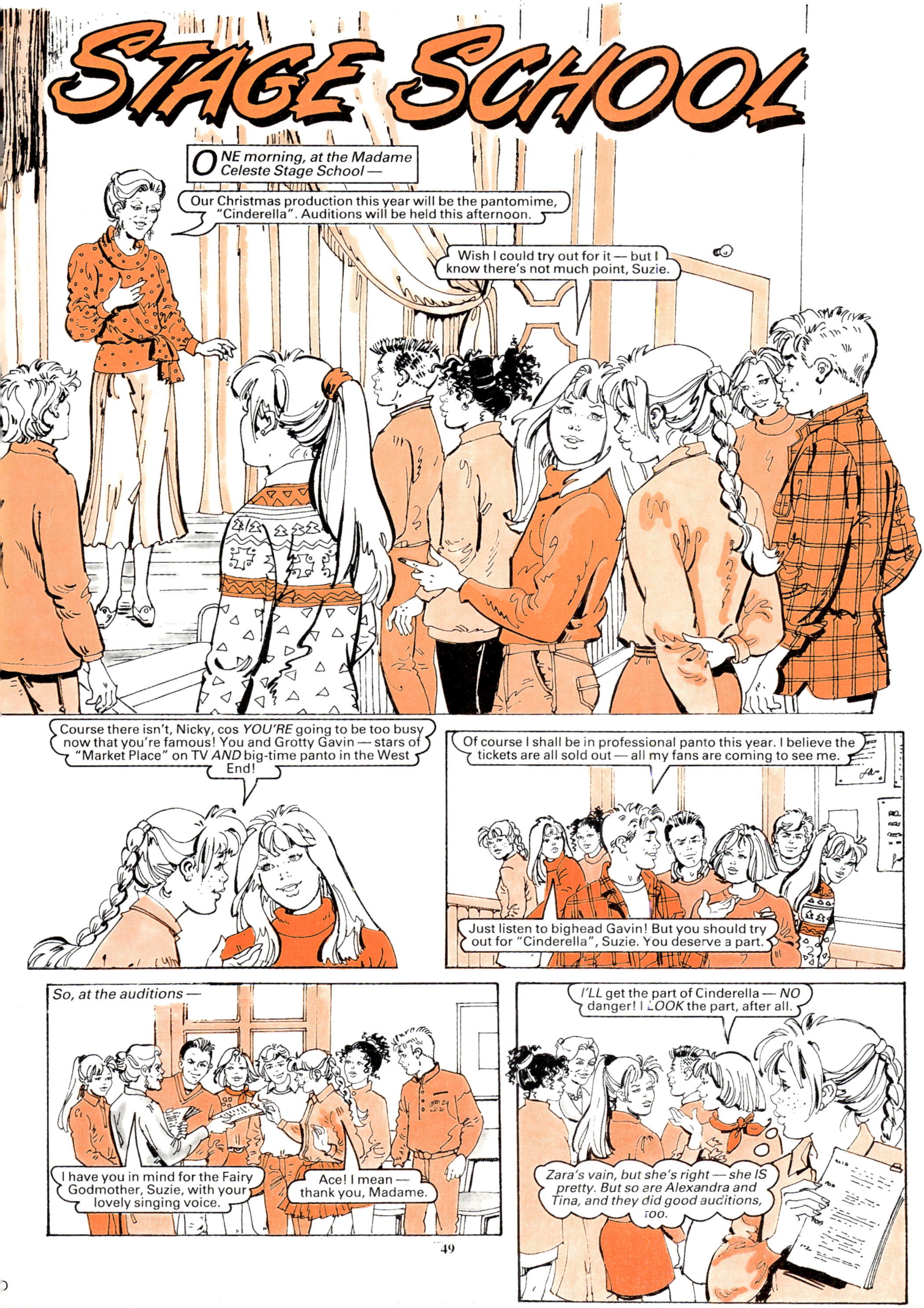

At last —
For Cinderella I have chosen Tina. In her reading, she brought out Cinderella's gentleness very well.
That's true. Zara and Alexandra are both a bit, well — posey. Tina will be good.
Later —
Well done, Tina! Good luck in the part!
Thank you, Suzie, but you shouldn't say that, you know. It's bad luck to wish someone good luck, and . . . oh!
My mirror! I've broken it . . . oh, dear! That's seven years' bad luck!
Oh, come on, Tina! You and your superstitions!
It's not superstition, Suzie. It's real — and VERY important.
Rehearsals began —
It's terrible, the way they make you slave for them, Cinders.
Oh, I don't mind hard work, Buttons. It's just . . .
Oh! Somebody's WHISTLING! Th-that's bad luck in the theatre!
Find out who it is, someone!

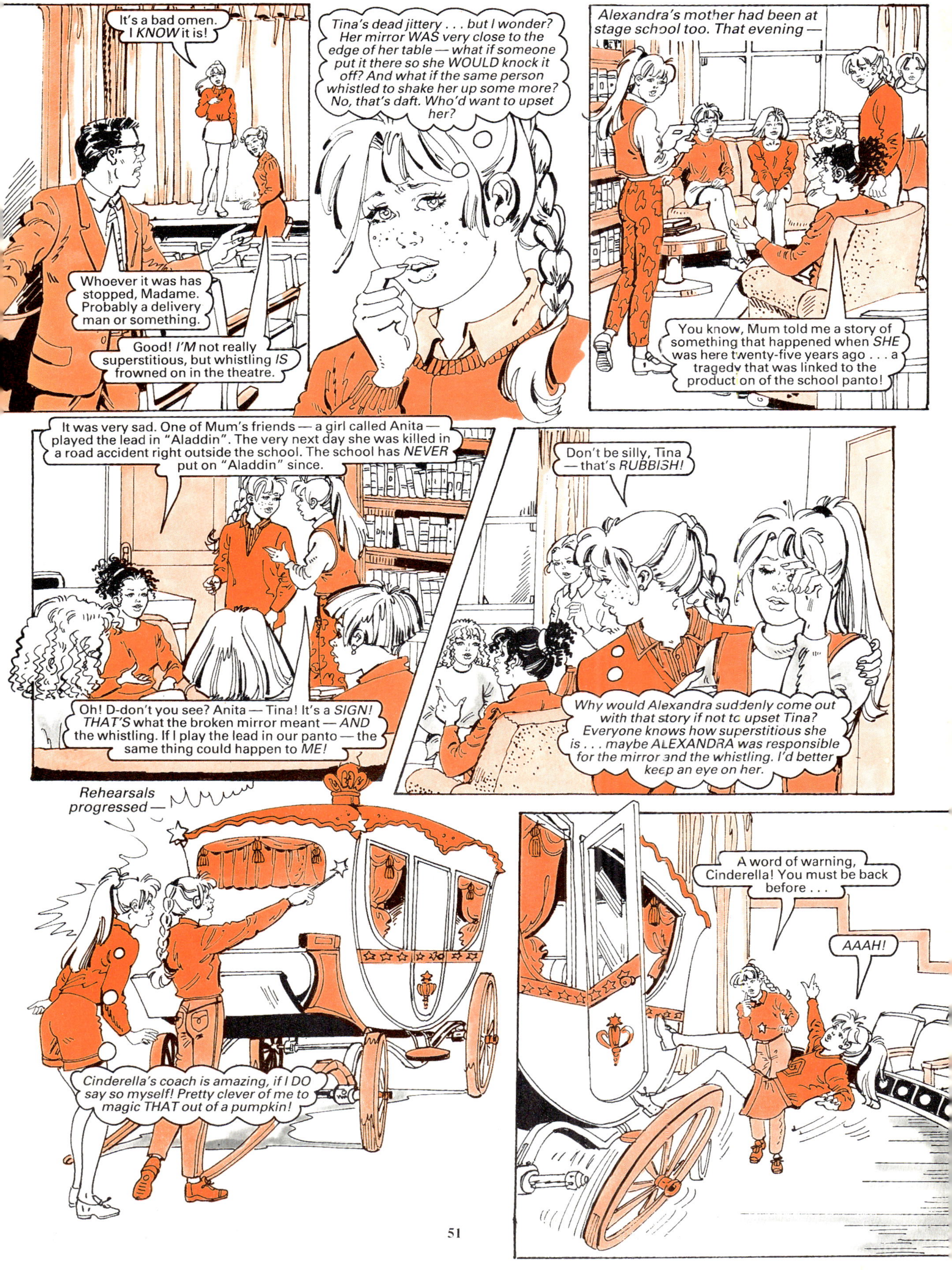
It's a bad omen. I KNOW it is!
Whoever it was has stopped, Madame. Probably a delivery man or something.
Good! I'M not really superstitious, but whistling IS frowned on in the theatre.
Tina's dead jittery . . . but I wonder? Her mirror WAS very close to the edge of her table — what if someone put it there so she WOULD knock it off? And what if the same person whistled to shake her up some more? No, that's daft. Who'd want to upset her?
Alexandra's mother had been at stage school too. That evening —
You know, Mum told me a story of something that happened when SHE was here twenty-five years ago . . . a tragedy that was linked to the production of the school panto!
It was very sad. One of Mum's friends — a girl called Anita — played the lead in "Aladdin". The very next day she was killed in a road accident right outside the school. The school has NEVER put on "Aladdin" since.
Oh! D-don't you see? Anita — Tina! It's a SIGN! THAT'S what the broken mirror meant — AND the whistling. If I play the lead in our panto — the same thing could happen to ME!
Don't be silly, Tina — that's RUBBISH!
Why would Alexandra suddenly come out with that story if not to upset Tina? Everyone knows how superstitious she is . . . maybe ALEXANDRA was responsible for the mirror and the whistling. I'd better keep an eye on her.
Rehearsals progressed —
Cinderella's coach is amazing, if I DO say so myself! Pretty clever of me to magic THAT out of a pumpkin!
A word of warning, Cinderella! You must be back before . . .
AAAH!

Are you all right, Tina?
Y-yes, Jamie . . .
Gracious, how could a wheel have come off the coach? Everything was perfectly secure at yesterday's rehearsal.
It's — it's another WARNING!
It's someone tampering with the coach! But it couldn't have been Alexandra cos she's away ill today. So SHE'S off the hook.
Next day —
Good, Zara. I'm pleased to see you studying your lines. The understudy for the lead role must always be word perfect, ready to step in at any time.
Oh! I hadn't realised that ZARA was understudying Tina! So maybe SHE'S the one trying to scare her out of the role? She's certainly the one who'd benefit!
And, at the next rehearsal —
EEEK!
Tina, are you hurt?
I — I could've been killed. I — I . . .
It was just an accident, Tina. The scenery toppled over, that's all.
I don't think the scenery was meant to hit Tina — just to miss her and scare her some more. Could Zara have done it?

After classes —
I've got to give up being Cinderella, Suzie. There's a curse on me! It's —
Watch where you're going, Tina!
TINA!
EEEK!
Y-you see? I nearly had an accident right outside the school — like poor Anita!
Of COURSE you nearly had an accident — cos you walked into the road without looking! That's NOTHING to do with a curse — you just weren't concentrating!
N-no! I'm going to step down from being Cinderella, before something REALLY terrible happens.
Listen, Tina, someone's playing nasty tricks on you to make you do just that — and I'll PROVE it!
Next day —
Been shopping, Suzie?
Yes, I've been down the market — and I've got a surprise for Tina.
An old horseshoe! They're supposed to be DEAD lucky! That's ACE, Suzie!
I've borrowed a hammer and nails from the caretaker and we'll nail it up above your bed. Then NO bad luck can touch you.

That's right, Suzie — nail it with the ends pointing up.
I'm not getting them in very far cos the wall's so hard. They feel a bit loose. I'll ask the caretaker to do it properly after supper. It'd be terrible if the top two nails fell out, cos the horseshoe'd swing downwards and *THAT'S* terribly *UNLUCKY*.
Supper's ready!
Great! Come on, Tina — I'm *STARVING!*
But outside the dorm, Suzie held her friend back.
Wait, Tina. I want to see if anyone's fallen into my trap!
TRAP?
Yes, a trap! I know *SOMEONE* was trying to scare you — and wouldn't be able to resist taking out a couple of nails.
It — it's *ZARA!*
You *CREEP*, Zara! When you saw how a couple of accidents and Alexandra's Aladdin story frightened Tina you decided to try and make her *SO* scared she'd give up her role! How *COULD* you?
Huh! I'd be *FAR* better as Cinderella, anyway. So what are you going to do — sneak to Madame?
That will not be necessary. I have heard quite enough. Zara, come with me at once!

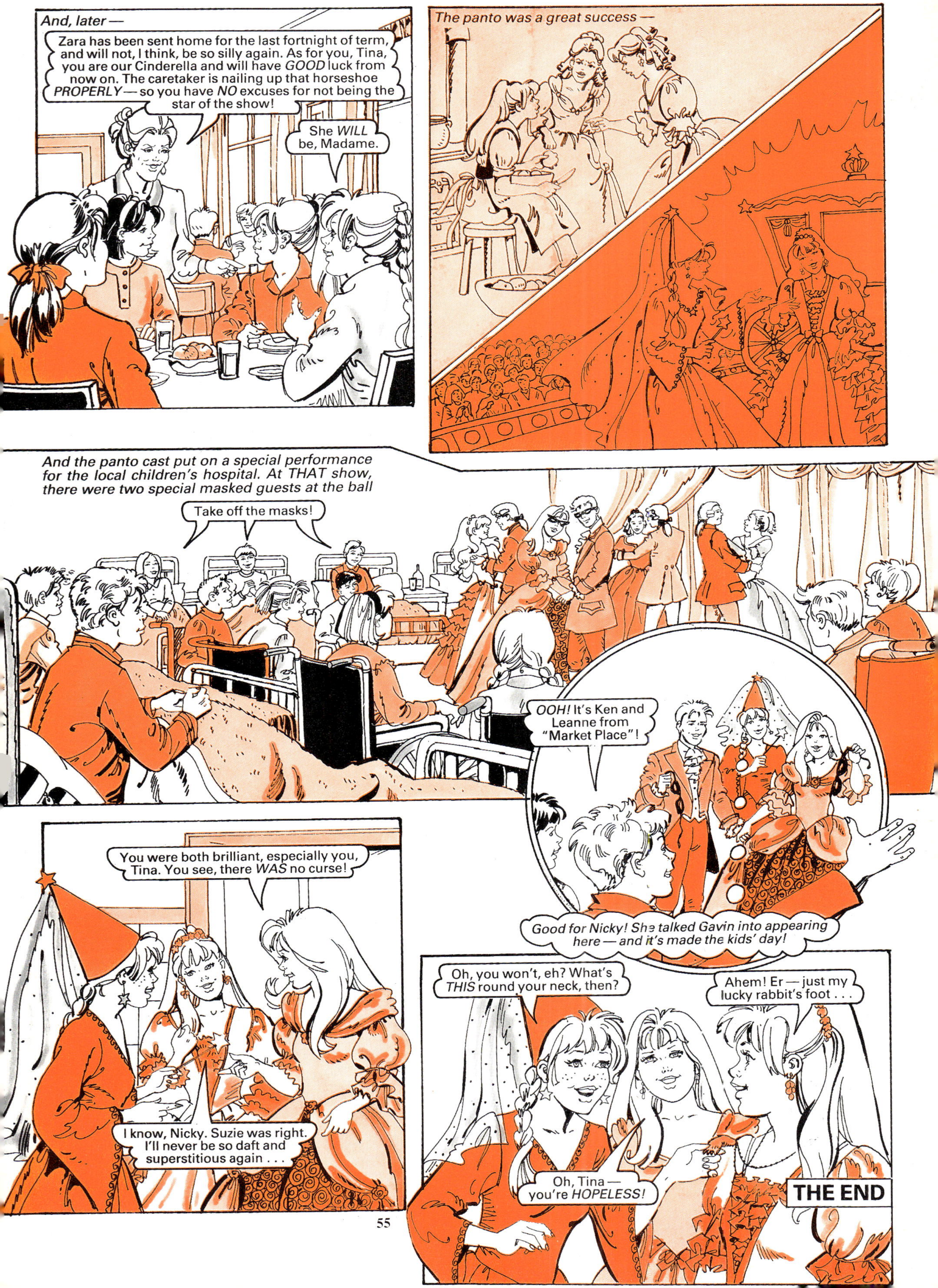

And, later —
Zara has been sent home for the last fortnight of term, and will not, I think, be so silly again. As for you, Tina, you are our Cinderella and will have GOOD luck from now on. The caretaker is nailing up that horseshoe PROPERLY — so you have NO excuses for not being the star of the show!
She WILL be, Madame.
The panto was a great success —
And the panto cast put on a special performance for the local children's hospital. At THAT show, there were two special masked guests at the ball
Take off the masks!
OOH! It's Ken and Leanne from "Market Place"!
Good for Nicky! She talked Gavin into appearing here — and it's made the kids' day!
You were both brilliant, especially you, Tina. You see, there WAS no curse!
I know, Nicky. Suzie was right. I'll never be so daft and superstitious again . . .
Oh, you won't, eh? What's THIS round your neck, then?
Ahem! Er — just my lucky rabbit's foot . . .
Oh, Tina — you're HOPELESS!
THE END

The Honourable SJ

Ah! I see just the person to look after you, Cynthia.
Miss Norton must mean S.J.
But—
Ann is in your dormitory, Cynthia. I'm sure she'll be happy to show you around.
Oh — certainly, Miss Norton.
S.J. looks furious! But she daren't make a scene.
Have you come far, Cynthia?
No. My family have recently bought the Cobden Estate quite near here.
I know it. It's HUGE!
They'd prefer me to go to a school further away — possibly abroad — so I'm only here temporarily.
You'll enjoy your stay. Millford's a nice place.
If you forget about S.J.!
Ann showed Cynthia around—
This is the tennis court. I play a bit now and then.
Great! Fancy a game, Ann?
So—
Great shot, Ann! You'll win easily!
Oh, no! I've broken a string.
No prob. Take my spare racquet.
Soon—
Well done! I told you you'd beat me!
I couldn't have done it without your racquet. Thanks for the loan of it.

Keep it. I've several more at home.
I couldn't! It's an expensive one, Cynthia!
Of course you can! We're friends, aren't we? I *WANT* to give it to you!
In that case — thanks.
Why are you putting that racquet in your locker, Smith?
It's mine, S.J. Cynthia gave it to me.
WHAT? It's far too good for you! Cynthia's more *MY* type than yours, and I intend to see that she becomes *MY* friend.
Trust S.J. to spoil things!
In the tuck shop—
Here you are, Cynthia — lemonade and doughnuts.
Thanks! M'mm! I hope they have lots of jam.
Mind if I join you? I couldn't help noticing this letter had arrived for Cynthia and I know how welcome letters from home are when you're new.
Thanks!
Not at all. It's a prefect's job to help new girls settle in.
When there's something in it for HER!
This looks interesting.
My father has written about a special reception that's to be held soon. I'll be allowed to leave to attend with him and I can invite a friend from school, too.
How nice!
I'll bet S.J. wants to be the one who's invited.
Sure enough, next day—
Go and tidy my study, Smith!
But I've arranged to meet Cynthia.

Tough luck! I want my study tidied and you'd better do it! I'll meet Cynthia in your place.
It's not fair, but there's nothing I can do about it. One word from S.J. to her father and Dad could lose his job and our cottage.
Hello, Cynthia! I've just seen Ann getting the bus to town.
But — but I've been waiting for her! We were going to go for a walk together.
She IS a bit unreliable — but never mind. I'll come with you.
Cynthia's bound to be annoyed at Ann. I'm sure I'll get the invitation now.
But—
I'm sorry about this afternoon, Cynthia.
That's all right — just a misunderstanding. It doesn't matter.
Bother! That stupid Cynthia is still friendly with Ann. I couldn't bear it if the daughter of one of Daddy's employees went to the reception instead of me. I MUST put her out of the running!
Next day—
Ann's year are all at lessons now, but I have a free period. I'll have a look in Cynthia's locker . . .
Ah! This is what I want. This brooch must be worth a fortune. Cynthia will be gobsmacked when she finds it's missing.
That evening—
Miss Norton has asked me to do a locker inspection.
Will we get a detention if our lockers are untidy, S.J.?
Of course not! I'm not that unkind, Sally.
S.J.'s great! Most prefects wouldn't miss a chance to give out punishments!
Everyone here thinks S.J. is perfect. If only they knew it's all an act.

Your lockers are fine. You can all go now.
Why has she come here? There MUST be a reason!
Oh, Cynthia! Is that a jewel box in your locker?
Yes, S.J.
You're supposed to hand in jewellery to the headmistress to keep. It's a Millford rule.
I didn't realise. The only really valuable thing I have is a ruby brooch. I'll take it to the Head's office straight away.
Oh! It's not here!
Someone must have taken it! The most likely person is someone from this dorm. I'll search all the lockers and beds.
Is this the brooch?
Yes. But . . . but that's *ANN'S* bed!
I thought you were my friend, Ann!
Scholarship girls like Ann can't be trusted, Cynthia.
I've been set up, but I can't say anything!
I don't want to cause trouble, so I won't report this to a teacher. But thank you for helping me to find out the truth about Ann, S.J. Will you come to the reception with me, as a "thank you"?
You bet, Cynthia!

Later—
What a day! I managed to get you into Cynthia's bad books and me into her good ones at the same time — AND I'm going to her swanky party!
You're horrible, S.J.! YOU took that brooch and planted it under my pillow.
So what? You can't say anything or your father will lose his job and cottage. You're in my power, Ann and don't you forget it!
Whatever S.J. wants, S.J. gets!
I heard that! So Ann was innocent after all. Ooh! I'm going all out to teach S.J. a lesson she won't forget.
Next day—
Tell me about the reception, Cynthia. Is it going to be very grand?
Terribly! There will even be a king and queen there.
And the food will be the very best. It's at the palace, you know.
Sounds wonderful! I'd better buy a new dress.
So—
It's the dearest in the shop. I'll be broke for the rest of term, but I must look special if I'm to meet royalty.
And, on the day—
We're ready to go to the party, Jenks.
Very good, Miss Cynthia.
Bet you wish YOU were going, Smith, but the company will be far above your class!

But—
20 · JOHN WHISTLER &
Where are we going? This is a common, rough district. I can't see a palace!
Oh, it's here all right, just around the corner.
BERT BROWN'S FISH & CHIP PALACE
Here we are — Bert Brown's Fish And Chip Palace! Dad's invited us to the opening of his latest branch.
OPENING TODAY!
My father is Bert Brown — *SIR* Bert, actually. He was knighted for his services to the catering industry. Dad, this is S.J.
Hello, Cynth, my darling! Bring your mate inside.

What'll you 'ave — fish and chips or jellied eels?
How common!
And here's the king and queen — a PEARLY king and queen, straight from the East End!
Wotcha, sweetheart! 'Ave a jellied eel!
Certainly not! I — there has been some mistake! I'm leaving!
Coo! Hoity-toity!
AAAH!

Well, S.J. It seems you *HAVE* fallen for the jellied eels after all!
Now, Cynth, no need to be nasty. She's 'ad a bit of a shock. Best fetch a doctor.
Next day at school—
. . . and you should have seen S.J.'s face! She was furious, Ann! Now she's in hospital with a broken ankle. Serves her right.
I'm so glad you found out it wasn't me who took your brooch, Cynthia — but S.J. never forgets or forgives. She'll try to get her own back on you.
She doesn't worry me. I'm leaving at the weekend for a school in Switzerland. But, before I go, I want to invite you to the *REAL* reception. It's at Cobden Manor on Thursday.
And so—
This is wonderful — to think I'm sitting next to a TV star! I'm sorry Cynthia's leaving Millford tomorrow. And S.J. will be even nastier when she gets out of the hospital. But at least Cynthia helped me to get the better of her — FOR ONCE!
THE END

DREAM BOY

MYRA ROSS wanted a boyfriend. The trouble was, boys never seemed to notice Myra. It was a different story for her best friend, Carrie.
See you later, Myra. Tom's asked me to go to the café with him and the gang.
Oh — well, have a nice time, Carrie.
Why didn't anyone ask ME to go along? Am I the Amazing Invisible Girl or something?
'Dream Boy'? Looks as if that new mag could help me. I'll order a copy to be delivered.
DREAM BOY
FOR GIRLS WHO ARE SEARCHING FOR THE BOY OF THEIR DREAMS.
FIRST ISSUE ON FRIDAY

So, on Friday morning —
Hi! Have you got my magazine there?
Yes — but what's the big hurry? Most people wait till I put the papers through the letterbox!
This is it! 'Dream Boy' is going to change my life! There's an advice column inside on how to find the boy of your dreams.
DREAM BOY
The advice this week says, 'To find any sort of boy at all, let alone your dream boy, you must go where boys are likely to be. What better place than a football match? Boys like girls who share their interests.'
I've never been to a football match in my life, but there's always a first time. I'll see if I can get Carrie to go with me.
You want me to go to the football with you on Saturday, Myra? But why? I didn't know you were a sports fan.
Oh — er — yes — I always watch it on telly. I'd like to see it for real, though. Come on, Carrie — it'll be fun.
Carrie agreed, and that Saturday —
You're not actually going to buy one of those daft rosette things, are you?
Yes — why not? I want to look like a really loyal supporter. Anyway, this light green goes with my outfit.
I can see a gang of boys from our class going in. It'll be ace if we can get to stand near them.
I hope we're not going to regret this, Myra!

Look, Carrie, we're right next to Gary and his mates from school!
Not looking too friendly, though, are they?
The match started. Soon —
GOAL!
I'm getting quite carried away with this football stuff. I mustn't forget that I'm here to find my dream boy, though.
But —
BOO! Why don't you stand with your own lot? Traitor!
Are they shouting at ME, Carrie?
Gerrout of it! Boo!
I don't understand it! I cheered for the goal, didn't I? I even bought a rosette.
Yes — green to match your outfit . . .
You don't seem to have noticed that the lads are all wearing dark green and white stripes! You've been cheering for the visiting team, you dope!
OH, NO!
They left quickly, and —
Do me a favour — next time you fancy going to a football match, ask some OTHER mug to go with you! 'Bye, Myra.
'Bye.
I didn't find my dream boy — and what a nightmare that football match turned out to be.

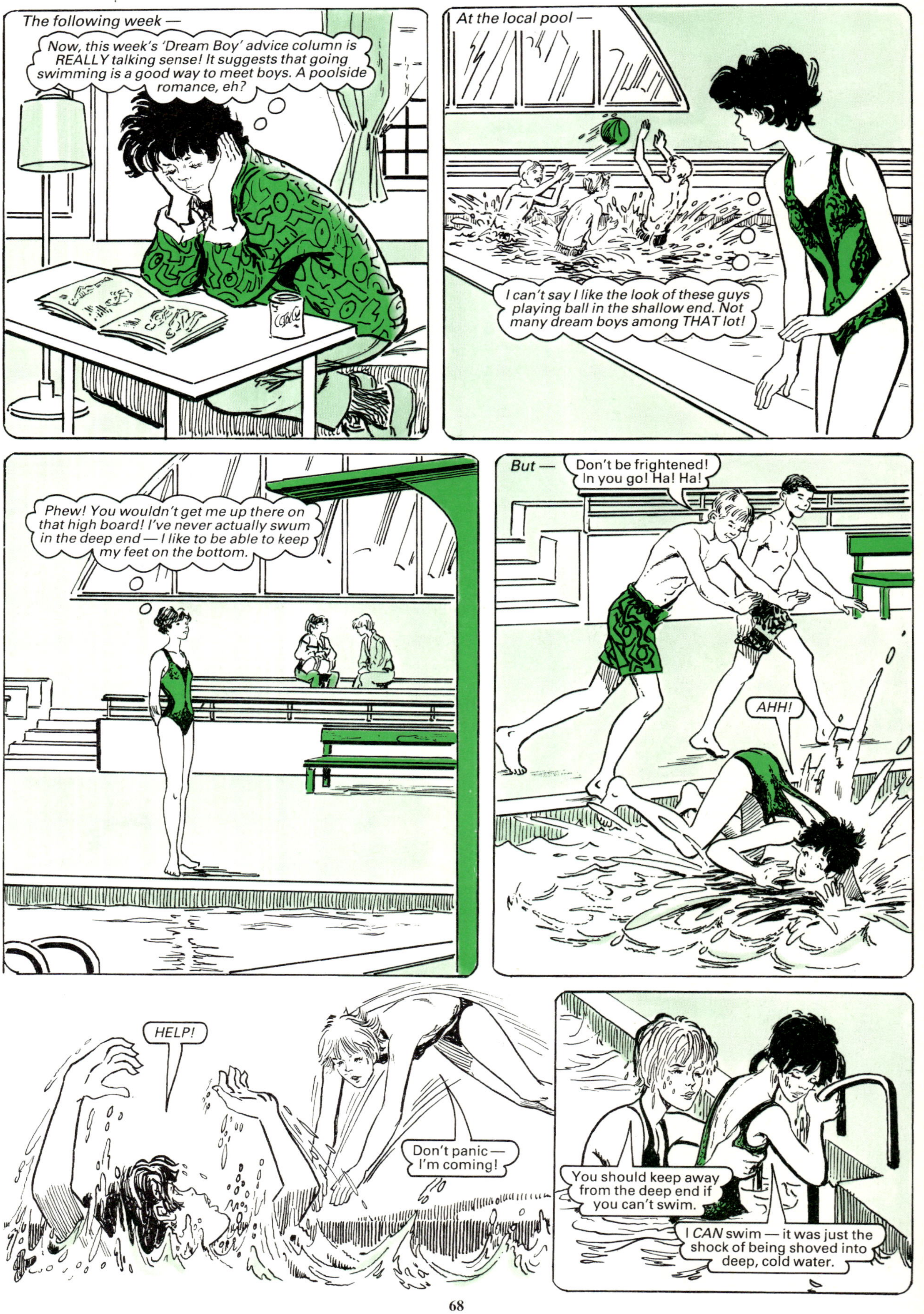
The following week —
Now, this week's 'Dream Boy' advice column is REALLY talking sense! It suggests that going swimming is a good way to meet boys. A poolside romance, eh?
At the local pool —
I can't say I like the look of these guys playing ball in the shallow end. Not many dream boys among THAT lot!
Phew! You wouldn't get me up there on that high board! I've never actually swum in the deep end — I like to be able to keep my feet on the bottom.
But —
Don't be frightened! In you go! Ha! Ha!
AHH!
HELP!
Don't panic — I'm coming!
You should keep away from the deep end if you can't swim.
I CAN swim — it was just the shock of being shoved into deep, cold water.

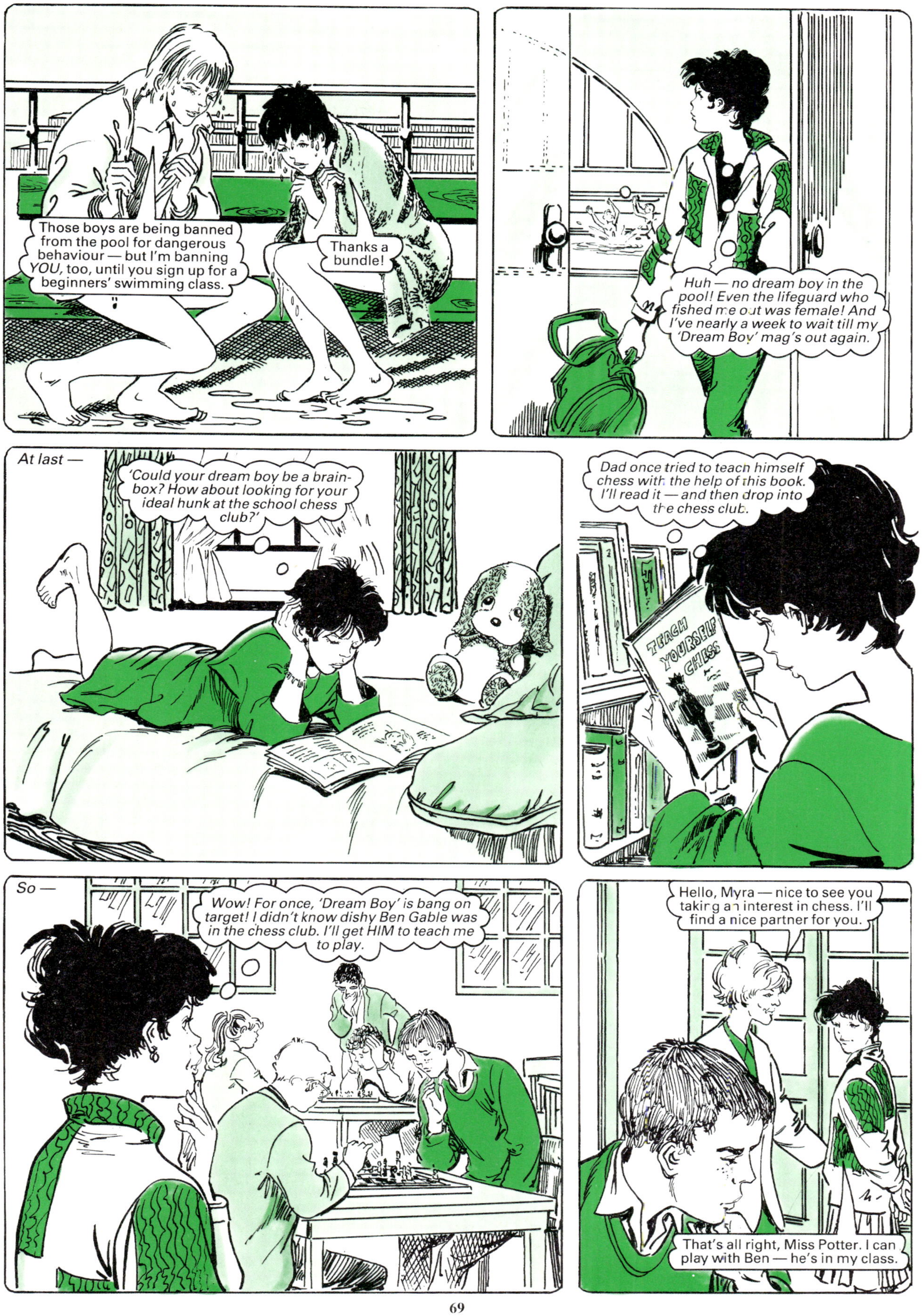
Those boys are being banned from the pool for dangerous behaviour — but I'm banning YOU, too, until you sign up for a beginners' swimming class.
Thanks a bundle!
Huh — no dream boy in the pool! Even the lifeguard who fished me out was female! And I've nearly a week to wait till my 'Dream Boy' mag's out again.
At last —
'Could your dream boy be a brain-box? How about looking for your ideal hunk at the school chess club?'
Dad once tried to teach himself chess with the help of this book. I'll read it — and then drop into the chess club.
TEACH YOURSELF CHESS
So —
Wow! For once, 'Dream Boy' is bang on target! I didn't know dishy Ben Gable was in the chess club. I'll get HIM to teach me to play.
Hello, Myra — nice to see you taking an interest in chess. I'll find a nice partner for you.
That's all right, Miss Potter. I can play with Ben — he's in my class.

Ben's already playing a game, dear. But Nigel hasn't got a partner, so play with him. He's quite an expert.
Oh, no! Swotty Simkins!
Now, Myra — I'm going to demonstrate to you seven great opening moves. You might like to take some notes.
Look Swot — er — Nigel — can't we just get on with it? I'm not aiming to be a world-class player.
An hour later —
No, no! Myra! How many times must I tell you that this piece is called the knight — NOT the 'horsie'!
You needn't tell me any more times, Swotty — I'm CHECKING out!
Myra was fed-up! On Friday —
Hang on — you can take that thing back to the shop, thanks very much. What's more, you can ask the newsagent to cancel my order.
I'm not surprised. I always thought you were far too bright to read that sort of rubbish. By the way — are you free on Saturday? I've got two tickets for a big rock concert.
Y-yes — wow! I'd love to go!
Great! See you on Saturday, then!
Why have I never noticed before how good-looking HE is?
I'm binning my back copies of 'Dream Boy' — and their useless advice. They missed out the best advice of all — 'Don't overlook the boy right under your nose.'
DREAM BOY
THE END

Hold That Tiger!
KATHY PERKINS had just put an advert in the newsagent's window.
I hope this will earn me some spare money for our holiday. It shouldn't be too hard anyway, cos I like animals.
Miss KATHY PERKINS (PET SITTER) DOGS, CATS, BUDGIES HAMSTERS (SORRY NO MICE) CARED FOR BY THE HOUR. TEL: 23976
FLA TO LET Apply
Kathy's first job was for the following Saturday.
Well, this should be easy enough. All I have to do here is look after a valuable cat while its owners spend a few hours at a friend's wedding.
Oh, it's the girl to look after Tiger. Come on in, dear. I'm glad you came early because we have to be at the church by ten o'clock, not half-past as I told you over the telephone.
My wife ALWAYS gets the time wrong!

We've no time to argue now, darling. We're late as it is. Tiger's in the kitchen, having his morning milk. We won't be long, dear. Bye!
Er, goodbye! Have a nice time!
Ah, here's Tiger. I'd better be careful not to startle him. Mrs Campbell said he was a nervous animal.
!
TIGER
Oh, no! I didn't think he'd be THAT nervous! I know I'm a stranger, but I AM here to look after him. I'd better catch him before he disappears completely.
Oh, help! I'll have to go after him! The Campbells would never forgive me if I lost their valuable cat!
But—
Oh, no! I'll NEVER catch Tiger now!

By the time Kathy got over the wall—
I knew it — he's disappeared! But I wonder if those dogs know something I don't? It's worth a look, anyway.
I was right! THERE'S Tiger! I've GOT to rescue him!
Go away! Go on — clear off!
Hey! That's no way to treat poor, dumb animals!
Poor, dumb animals, eh? Just look how much they've frightened poor Tiger! How on earth am I going to get him down from there?
Humph! That's YOUR problem!
The Campbells will go spare if Tiger gets hurt! I suppose I'd better get up there after him.

Thank goodness I'm not wearing a skirt! Now if I can just — oh, no!
HELP!
DRAT that cat!
Ooh . . . where am I? What happened? What's that funny noise?
YEOWL . . .
Oh, no! Tiger's DROWNING! I MUST save him!

Got you, Tiger. Now just hold still till I get us both on to dry land.
Cats can be VERY ungrateful!
Ouch, Tiger — that HURT! Oh, no! Come BACK!
By the time Kathy put her shoes on again, Tiger had completely vanished.
I haven't a clue where he is. All I can do now is go back to the Campbells' house — and hope Tiger turns up before THEY do!
Just then—
Hey, wait a minute! There's an awful noise coming from that fish shop — and cats LOVE fish! Maybe it's Tiger!
FISHMONG
Scram, you brute! How dare you steal my fish!
SALMON
TROUT
Tiger! Stop!
Got you — oh!
Yours, is he, miss? Well, you're due me the price of a cod, then.
By the time Kathy paid up—
Oh, no! Every cat in the district is after Tiger and the fish!

Kathy needn't have worried. Tiger headed straight home.
Great! Tiger's obviously decided that's the best way to make sure he keeps his fish!
Kathy chased off the other cats and—
SLAM!
Whew! What a long day this has been. I think I deserve a cup of tea.
Hello, dear. Had a nice day? How's our Tiger?
Oh, he's fine, Mrs Campbell.
Suddenly—
Take that, you flea-bitten beast! Get out of my kitchen! OUT!
Eh?
TIGER
Ah, here's our Tiger. Hello, pussikins. Has this nice girl been looking after you, then?
I don't believe it — I've spent all morning chasing after the WRONG cat! And ANYTHING could've happened to the REAL Tiger while I was gone!
There, dear. You've done a wonderful job. We'll let you know next time Tiger needs looking after. You've obviously taken GREAT care of him today.
Kathy headed for the newsagent's —
MISS KATHY PERKINS BABYSITTER Tel: 23976
CAR FOR SALE VW 8963
FUR COAT
FLAT
REPAIR UNDER
I've decided to look after CHILDREN instead. They're bound to be less bother. I don't think I could stand another CAT-astrophic day like that!
THE END

The Boy Zone

LAUREN had been going out with Spider for a few weeks. One night, at Lauren's house —
Look, Spider! They're advertising that new Domino jewellery range. It's really eye-catching. I love it!
The model's pretty eye-catching, too — dark and mysterious — everything I'm NOT. But as long as Spider likes ME, that's all that matters.
But, when Lauren spoke to Spider —
SPIDER!
He's so engrossed he isn't hearing me! The Domino Girl certainly seems to have caught HIS eye!
Later —
I can't wait for the school hols, Lauren. We'll be able to go out together every day.
So much for glam girls on TV — Spider only fancies ME!

But a couple of days later, round at Spider's —
Spider, that advert you like is on now!
Ace! Won't be a sec, Lauren.
WHAT advert?
The Domino Girl! Huh!
Am I REALLY the girl for you, Spider? Maybe you'd prefer someone more exotic, like the girl in the Domino ad.
No, you're everything I want, Lauren. And I bet YOU'D look as good as her with all the make-up and hair people she's got helping her.
Meaning I DON'T look as good now?
Oh, leave it, Lauren. You're my girl — okay?
Okay.
Sounds as if he means it!
On Saturday —
Won't be long, Lauren, then we'll go to the café. I'm just setting the video recorder.
Tom's on the phone, Spider!
Spider's set just a couple of minutes at a time. I don't believe it! He's recording the ADVERTS — to see the Domino Girl again!

In the café —
Guess what? I got you a gingerbread teddy.
HOT ... TEA COFFEE
Spider can be so sweet. It's hard to believe he's hankering after someone else. Maybe I've got it wrong. It may SEEM that he's fallen in love with the Domino Girl, but things are rarely black and white — apart from Domino jewellery!
Here, have a button off the teddy. They're choccy chips.
Thanks. Listen, do you mind if I don't go round the shops with you this afternoon? There's something I've got to do at home. I'll see you tonight.
Two hours later, Lauren was heading home when —
Oh! I've just remembered — I told Mum I'd buy that magazine she wanted.
BUS STOP
In the newsagent's —
There's SPIDER! But he SAID he was going home hours ago! And why's he looking at GIRLS' mags?
WOMEN
Lauren stayed out of sight and, when Spider had gone —
DOMINO
He BOUGHT this one! And I know why! It's got a full-page advert of the DOMINO GIRL! Well, I've had enough — I'm telling him we're FINISHED! He'll probably never even get to MEET the Domino Girl, but I'm still not playing second best like this!

At Spider's —
Hi, Lauren! Spider's doing something out in the shed. Just go round, dear.
Huh! Why does glue always stick to what you DON'T want — like your fingers?
What's he doing? Making a scrapbook of Domino Girl pics?
Then Lauren got a closer look —
Oh! Now I see! I — er — think I'd better just sneak off home!
And, that evening —
A present? For ME?
Be careful opening it, Lauren.
Wow! A necklace — just like the one the Domino Girl wears! I LOVE it!
I MADE it for you, Lauren. Nice, isn't it? But what a job I had getting hold of a good picture of the thing to copy from!
THE END

WELCOME TO MANDY m&J JUDY

FOR FUN-LOVIN' GIRLIES!

Sally-Ann Barber, Maidstone

Catherine Bell, Bingley

Victoria Chapman, Pinner

Nicola Barry, Newbridge

Katy Teo, Carluke

Emma Crowe, Newbury (fun-lovin'?!)

Becky Hill, Stow-on-the-Wold

Starscope

WHAT 1995 HOLDS FOR *YOU!*

CAPRICORN

(Dec 23-Jan 22)

LURRVE Roll on the summer months! That's when you'll meet the guy of your dreams. He's got the lot — good looks, nice nature — what MORE could you want?

LUCK Luck is definitely on the side of you Capricorn girlies. A good year lies ahead of you — so enjoy.

LIFE Some probs at school this year — but nothing you can't cope with. October looks set to be a wow of a month.

AQUARIUS

(Jan 23-Feb 19)

LURRVE A mate of yours has her eyes on the same guy as you fancy — BIG probs! Don't worry — you'll both find out he's not worth your attention.

LUCK You'll increase your luck as the months go by if you try to wear green, your lucky colour, as much as possible.

LIFE The Olds might lose patience with your untidiness, so why not give 'em a break? Start the new year with a sparkling, tidy room.

PISCES

(Feb 20-March 21)

LURRVE Watch out! Cupid's arrow is aimed at you. You'll fall for a luvverly guy and then it will be fun, fun, fun all the way.

LUCK This is your year to get lucky. Changing your image will help you to do it, so what's stopping you?

LIFE No doubt that squids — or the lack of 'em — could cause you probs on and off all year. Try being more careful.

ARIES

(March 22-April 20)

LURRVE There's a lotta partying around for you this festive season. Look out for THAT special kiss under the mistletoe.

LUCK A win is on the cards, so enter every competition you can and you could be a REAL lucky winner!

LIFE Easter will be your fave time this year — not only because of choccie eggs. Something extra-special will happen then.

TAURUS

(April 21-May 21)

LURRVE Come on — this year you can do it! ASK him out! He can only say 'no' — but he won't. He likes you, too.

LUCK The number thirteen will have great significance for you all year — so look out for it!

LIFE You will grow more than you banked on this year so keep some squids back for the loadsa new gear you'll need.

TENNIS STAR ANDRE AGASSI (APRIL 29th)

GEMINI

(May 22-June 21)

LURRVE An outing in a foursome won't go as well as you hoped. Not to worry — you'll find a new guy before the year's end.

LUCK All your luck will land towards the end of the year — so don't give up looking for it.

LIFE Winter will be your happiest season. The snow and frost won't bother you. By December you'll be having a great time, lucky thing.

CANCER

(June 22-July 23)

LURRVE The stars all point to a guy arriving in your life in autumn. It looks like he'll be around for a long time.

LIFE A lucky find will bring you loads MORE luck, a new friend and some new interests — SOME year!

LUCK Around Hallowe'en an invitation will have you looking for a fancy dress costume — watch out for the ghosties!

FILM STAR CHRISTIAN SLATER (AUGUST 18th)

LIBRA

(Sept 24-Oct 23)

LURRVE Dark-haired guys, fair-haired guys, red-haired guys — the choice is yours! You're going to be mega-popular all year long.

LUCK To increase your luck, try keeping your diary up-to-date and check every entry so that you're not double-booked.

LIFE When the festive season's here you'll be hip-hop-happy every day — but ESPECIALLY on the day a surprise pressie arrives.

SCORPIO

(Oct 24-Nov 22)

LURRVE Don't look too keen or you'll put someone off. Play it cool and everything will work out this year just as you hope.

LUCK Your luck will lie in your ability to go with the flow. Try it and your good fortune will treble.

LIFE Remember, remember the fifth of November! This year, Guy Fawkes night will be EXTRA-special for you.

LEO

(July 24-Aug 23)

LURRVE Mum won't approve of that lad you fancy. Just wait — your mum will be proved right — but you'll find someone else.

LUCK That lucky black cat is ready to leap into your life in spring. Once he crosses your path you won't look back.

LIFE Holidays will be really out-of-the-ordinary for you this year. You'll have the time of your life!

VIRGO

(Aug 24-Sept 23)

LURRVE A newcomer to your area in spring will set your heart fluttering. Take loadsa time to decide if he's right for you.

LUCK Your luckiest month will be November. The stars will be in position to put sparkle into everything you do.

LIFE An important phase of your life is coming to an end this year. Don't be sad! It's the start of a mega new beginning.

SAGITTARIUS

(Nov 23-Dec 22)

LURRVE This year will end with the stars in your eyes doing cartwheels! HE will ask you to a Christmas disco or party.

LUCK Don't rush into everything at once. Take one step at a time and good luck will be with you ALL year.

LIFE A first-foot will cause changes in your life — NEXT year! Be ready for loadsa new happenin's.

make 'n' do

It's me again. Christmas is THE time for stuffing your face with choccies, but what about all the empty boxes? Turn them into something fabsy!

WELL SPOTTED

You'll need:- An old choccy box; paint.

What to do:

It's easy-peasy lemon-squeezy to turn a boring box into a handy holder for all your precious jewels. Simply paint the box outside and in to cover up the writing. We used pearl paints for a nice effect (available from toy departments or the Early Learning Centre) and decorated the box with spots. You can try any design you like. Why not try sticking on some pieces of ripped tissue (see MIRROR MAGIC on page 48)? Leave in one of the sweet trays and you have ready made compartments for earrings, brooches and rings.

WHAT A GEM

You'll need:- Matchbox; round box for cheese; plaster filler for walls (this comes powdered or ready mixed); gold or silver craft paint; stick on jewels.

What to do:

You can transform almost anything. The round box we used was a wooden one that had special cheese for Christmas in it, but a cardboard one that contained chunky cheese triangles works just as well. The matchboxes make especially good gift boxes for earrings.

First, give your boxes a coat or two of paint. When the paint is dry, put the filler on top (follow any instructions for mixing that are on the pack) and press the jewels lightly into it while it's still wet. Leave to dry thoroughly. Next, paint the filler with gold or silver paint. If you like, you can also paint a design on to the box and add some glitter for extra sparkle, and that's all there is to it.

HEART FELT

You'll need:- A sweetie box; some left-over wrapping paper; glue; scraps of tissue.

What to do:

This makes a lovely gift or trinket box (remember Mother's Day in March) and it's dead easy to do. Cover the box with some plain gift wrap and decorate it with shapes torn from the tissue. We used hearts, but you could also try flowers, triangles, stars or circles. It only takes minutes to make and we bet Mum would love to get a prez tied up in a box she could keep like this.

FEET FIRST

You'll need:- A shoe box; a small amount of household emulsion; poster paints; craft varnish.

What to do:

Get new shoes or slippers from Santa? Well, the box is just right for storing scrunchies, hair bands and ribbons. Paint the box and lid inside and out with the emulsion. If the Olds don't have any left-overs a sample size pot is ideal. You may need to give it two coats for a nice smooth finish. When the emulsion is dry, add a design with some contrasting paint. We chose a simple zig-zag design and painted it round the edges of the lid and the top and bottom edges of the box. To finish, cover the box with one or two coats of varnish. This stops the design rubbing and will make your box waterproof, so that you can wipe off dust or marks.

CUT IT OUT!

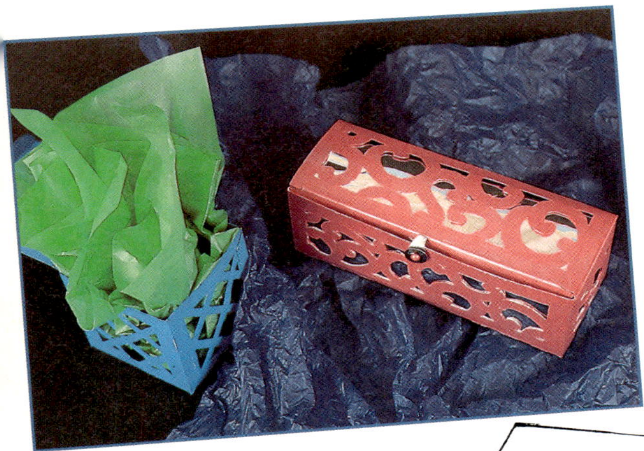

CUT OUT SHADED PARTS

You'll need:- A box; paint; scraps of foil wrap; scraps of ribbon; a button.

What to do:

These gift or trinket boxes are mega posh. First, carefully unstick the joins of the box so that you can lay it out flat. Draw a border round each section and then plan out your design (see diagram). You can choose a simple design like the criss-cross one or make a fancier, curved one. Now for the hard bit — you have to cut out sections round your design. We used a craft knife, but these are very sharp, so it may be best to get an Old to help you with this. When that's done, paint both sides of the box. If you want to add contrasting foil wrap to shine through, it's easiest to stick this to the wrong side of the box now. Give the right side a coat of craft varnish if you want a shiny finish.
Now you have to fold the box up again and restick the joins. To finish off, make a little fastener with a loop of ribbon and a button. Make a small hole in the centre front of the lid, thread the ribbon through to form a loop and secure with a knot on the wrong side. Tie the button on to the centre top of the front of the box.
If you haven't lined your box, wrap your gift in contrasting tissue for a grand, expensive effect.

You'll find some more fabsy ideas on page 93.

SEAN
MAGUIRE

MORE **PUZZLES** 'N' THINGS

ON THE BOX

Are you a telly addict or not? Here's the chance to put yourself to the test!

1. What part does Julia Sawalha play in Absolutely Fabulous?
2. Name this "Only Fools And Horses" actor.
3. Which member of the Addams Family is Jimmy Workman?
4. Complete this title. Beverly Hills -----.
5. Name the High School in "Saved By The Bell".
6. Name the actor who plays Clark Kent in "The New Adventures of Superman".
7. On which show are you most likely to meet "The Eliminator"?
8. Complete the names of these Baywatch bods. a) M-T- B-O-Y b) M-T-H B-C-A-N-N
9. Which soap is based in Weatherfield?
10. When should you turn on to see "The Big Breakfast"?
11. Can you name these "Birds Of A Feather"?

12. Which planet does Superman come from?
13. Name the very famous person Lenny Henry is married to.
14. Complete these cartoon titles: a) -H- ---NTSTO--- b) -U- -UNN- c) --OOB- -O-.
15. Name the very funny person who presented the series about safe driving.
16. Which programme did Napoleon and Illya appear in?
17. Name this TV dog.
18. In "The Street", who did Reg marry earlier this year?
19. Name "The Wonder Years" star.
20. Which soap would you be in if you were in Summer Bay?

All transparencies on this page — courtesy of BBC.

ANSWERS ON PAGE 112

NAME GAME

Below is a list of over 60 girls' names. Can you hunt them out? Names may be read forwards, backwards, up, down or diagonally. Letters may be used more than once.

A	M	Y	N	A	R	O	D	E	M	I	L	Y	P	O	N	L	J
T	N	A	E	J	G	L	O	O	E	L	A	C	E	P	A	A	A
I	B	N	L	W	K	Y	N	L	I	M	R	U	N	A	T	U	C
R	C	D	E	H	E	R	N	H	R	N	A	L	N	I	A	R	Q
T	E	N	H	G	L	E	A	C	R	I	S	S	Y	C	L	A	U
E	F	I	F	E	E	M	V	S	A	R	A	H	J	I	I	L	E
I	R	S	B	E	A	T	R	I	C	E	R	C	U	R	E	U	L
R	A	A	N	I	N	A	Y	J	C	N	B	A	L	T	N	A	I
R	N	B	N	G	O	D	D	U	A	E	E	R	I	A	U	P	N
A	C	E	E	G	R	N	N	D	H	H	L	O	E	P	J	E	E
H	E	L	R	A	E	E	A	Y	T	F	I	L	T	T	E	R	J
B	S	A	I	M	N	L	M	N	A	A	N	I	G	L	A	C	O
F	I	O	N	A	A	G	A	Y	C	A	D	N	I	Y	D	K	A
B	Z	T	C	Y	I	Y	T	T	A	P	A	E	M	M	A	E	N
E	O	I	N	E	D	B	E	B	E	O	H	P	Y	T	T	I	K
T	E	N	D	F	Y	S	T	A	P	B	E	S	I	U	O	L	I
H	E	A	J	I	L	L	I	M	O	A	N	L	O	R	N	A	B
J	E	S	S	I	C	A	N	O	I	R	A	M	N	E	R	A	K

ANNE	CATH	EILEEN	ISABEL	KITTY	MAGGIE	PAULA
AMY	CAROLINE	FAY	JACQUELINE	KATE	MARION	PATSY
ANGELA	CHLOE	FIONA	JOAN	KAREN	MERYL	PENNY
ANTHEA	DONNA	FRANCES	JENNY	LUCY	NINA	RAE
BEATRICE	DIANE	GLENDA	JILL	LAURA	NATALIE	RITA
BELINDA	DORA	GWEN	JESSICA	LOUISE	NAOMI	SARAH
BETH	EMILY	HELEN	JUDY	LYDIA	PHOEBE	SARA
CRISSY	ELEANOR	HARRIET	JULIET	LORNA	PATRICIA	TINA
CARRIE	EMMA	IRENE	JUNE	MANDY	PATTY	ZOE

ALPHABET quiz

Trivial Pursuit

Trivial Pursuit is a registered trademark of Horn Abbot International Ltd.

The Alphabet Quiz is really easy. The answer to the first question starts with an A and so on . . .

A Name the playing card with one diamond on it.
B Which very large wrestler's real name is Shirley Crabtree?
C Which city in England has the same name as a leather sofa?
D What compete for prizes at Crufts?
E What kind of animal is Dumbo?
F Which is the shortest month of the year?
G Who 'kissed the girls and made them cry'?
H What did Winnie the Pooh call elephants?
I What is the name of the spider that climbed up the spout?

J Who is the only person who could write Jason Donovan's autobiography?

K What is Barbie doll's boyfriend called?
L From what is the outside of a cricket ball made?
M What plant do people kiss under at Christmas?

N Name this well-known actress.

O What kind of trees grow from acorns?
P Which famous Phillip was born on April Fool's Day?
Q Name the noise a duck makes.

R Which Beano character always does his best to get out of doing things?

S Which hero does Lois Lane love?
T Which game calls 'deuce' when each player has 40 points?
U From which country do Cadillac cars come?
V What kind of card is sent on February 14th?
W What is the capital city of the USA?
X A type of photograph taken by a radiographer.
Y What is the name of the yellow part of an egg?
Z Name the crossing with the same name as an animal?

ANSWERS ON PAGE 112

READY, STEA

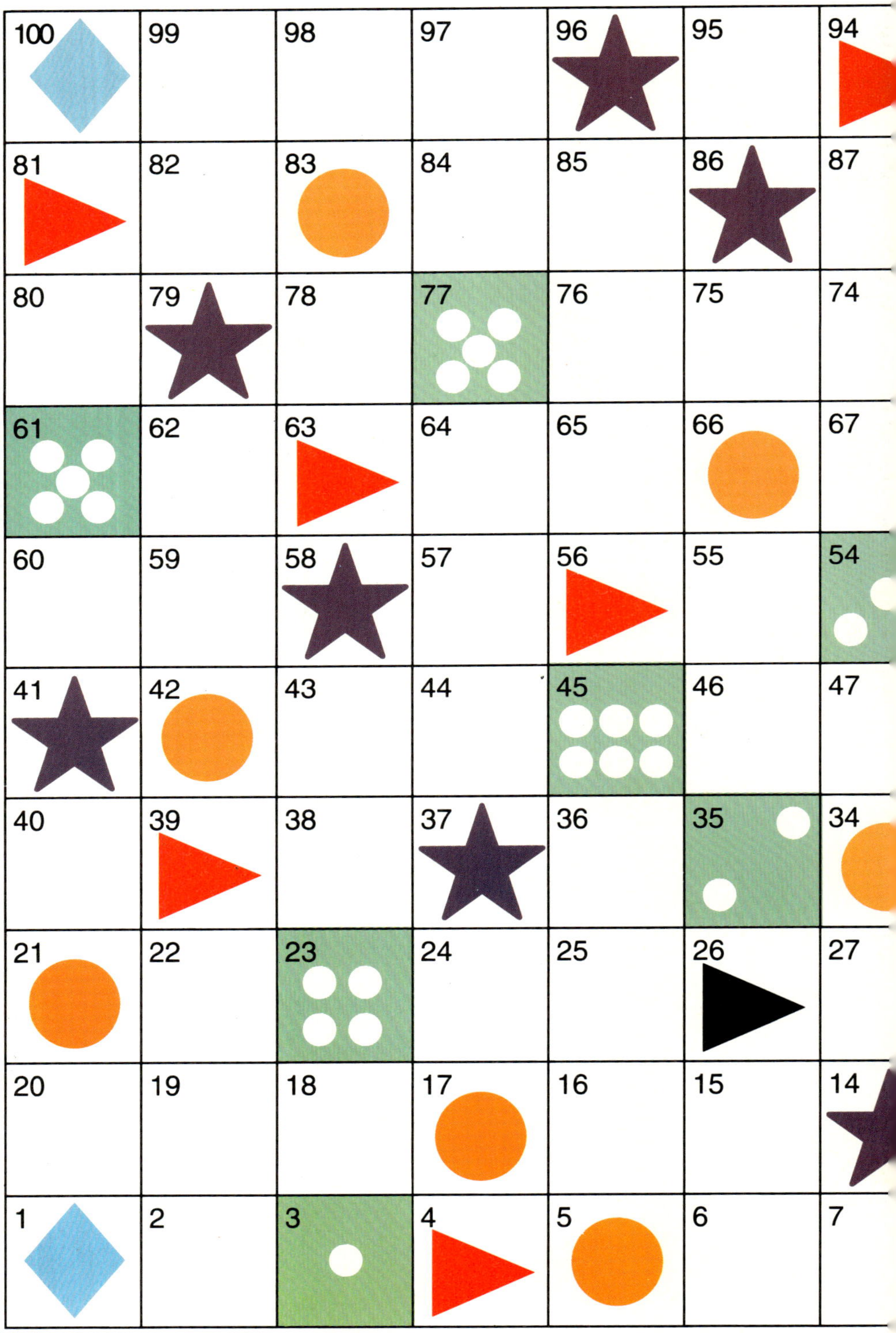

Here's a groovy game for you and your mates to play. All you need is a dice and something to use as game counters (such as old buttons or sweets).

Claire xx

ADY GO!

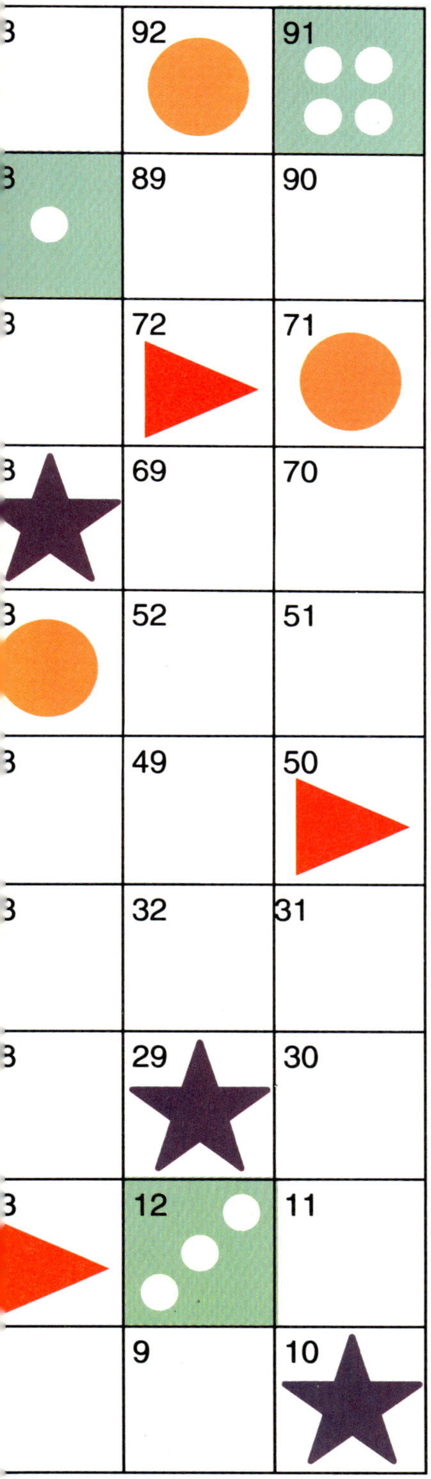

◆ HOW TO PLAY ◆

It's dead easy — throw a six to start and then work your way round the board.
If you land on a RED triangle go back 2 spaces.
If you land on an AMBER circle miss a turn.
If you land on a GREEN dice answer the next question from the GREEN dice section and then follow the instructions.
If you land on a PURPLE star go forward 1 space.
The winner is the first person to reach the end AND complete a test from the BLUE diamond section (your mates get to choose the test!).
Have fun!

1. Name all 5 members of Take That (first AND second names). If you answer correctly have another turn.
2. If you did your shopping at Alf's store and hung out at the Surf Club, which programme would you be in? Move forward 3 if you get it right.
3. There are 2 of them, they're Dutch and their hits include NO LIMITS, TRIBLE DANCE and FACES. Who are they? Go back 2 if you're wrong.
4. Who was the muscley star of LAST ACTION HERO? Right or wrong, stay where you are.
5. He used to play Henry in NEIGHBOURS, then released a few pop singles and went on to star in the stage version of GREASE. What's his name? Have another go if you're right.
6. They're creepy and they're kooky and really kinda spooky. Who are they? Right or wrong, stay there.
7. Robin Williams dressed up as an old lady for this film. What was it called? Move on 3 spaces if you get it right.
8. Who plays BLOSSOM? Miss your next turn if you get it wrong.
9. How many boys are in Bad Boys Inc? Move on four spaces if you're right.
10. Which wildly colourful puppet dudes can you see on THE BIG BREAKFAST? Right or wrong, stay where you are.
11. He's big 'n' pink 'n' fat and covered with yellow spots. Who is he? Have another turn if you're right.
12. Which town is HOME & AWAY set in? Go back 1 space if you don't know.
13. On which TV show would you meet Wolf, Cobra and Saracen? Move on 2 spaces if you're right.
14. How did East 17 get their name? Move forward 2 if you're right. Go back one space if you're wrong.
15. He's really ugly and she's beautiful. There's a baddie called Gaston and loadsa singing and dancing household objects. Which film are you watching? Right or wrong, stay where you are.
16. What's the name of the Australian band who think they're ABBA? Go forward 3 spaces if you get it right.
17. Who are the 2 crazy dudes who had an Excellent Adventure and then went on a Bogus Journey? Have another turn if you know the answer.
18. This BLOSSOM star is a pretty good singer. Who is he? Right or wrong, stay where you are.
19. What are the names of ROSEANNE'S daughters? Move on 2 if you're right. Go back 2 if not.
20. Which group have released albums called . . . AND PARTY! and EVERYTHING CHANGES? Miss a turn if you don't know.
21. What's the name of the guy who plays Superman in THE NEW ADVENTURES OF SUPERMAN? Move on 3 spaces if you're right.
22. Which programme was Sean McGuire in before he moved to EASTENDERS? Throw again if you're right.
23. Before Emma Forbes began presenting LIVE & KICKING she used to do something different on GOING LIVE. What was it? Right or wrong, stay where you are.
24. Which duck can be found in a broom cupboard? Have another go if you get the answer correct.
25. A crumblie old pop star sang with Take That on their RELIGHT MY FIRE single. Who was she? Go back 2 spaces if you're wrong.
26. What are the first names of the Minogue sisters? Throw a six to start again if you get it wrong.
27. In the film TOP GUN, what job did Tom Cruise have? Move forward one space if you know.
28. What is the real name of THE FRESH PRINCE OF BEL-AIR? Miss a turn if you're wrong.
29. When Kevin McAllister was left HOME ALONE the second time, where was he? Right or wrong, stay there.
30. In the film BEETHOVEN, what was Beethoven? Move forward 2 spaces if you get it right.

Complete one of these tests after you've reached 100 and you are a WINNER!

1. Stand in the middle of your garden and loudly sing a nursery rhyme.
2. Count to 10 in French.
3. Do 20 one-handed press-ups. Oh, okay then, you can use 2 hands. (Bet you still can't do it, though!)
4. Recite the alphabet backwards.
5. Put a cardi on backwards, put socks on your hands and run round the garden 3 times.

Answers on page 112.

DO THEY DIFFER?

See if you can spot the 20 differences between the two pictures below.

ANSWERS ON PAGE 112

make 'n' do

Back again! You just can't get rid of me. Here's the last of the Christmas recycling ideas showing how even the most useless looking, tatty old box can be transformed. Get busy!

YOU'VE BEEN FRAMED!

You'll need:- The cardboard flaps cut from the box; paints; craft glue; string, ribbon or cord; a fave piccie.

What to do:

Make loads of these brill photo frames for all your fave pics. Cut one of the flaps into four strips. You'll need to make them all the same width — 4 or 5 cm is ideal. Position them over your photo to get a guide size and then glue them together so that they form a square or rectangle (the shape depends on your photo). Trim the overlapping edges so that they all measure the same.
Paint the frame any colour you like. You can paint all the strips a different colour or paint the top and bottom with one colour and the sides with another. We used a circle stencil cut from card to add detail — just gently dab on some contrasting paint with a piece of sponge. You could also decorate frames to match your storage boxes using the crumpled paper method. Coat your frame with clear craft varnish to make it harder. Tie some coloured string (or paint plain string to match), ribbon or cord round the corners to finish. Stick your pic to the back and that's that!

SUPER STORE

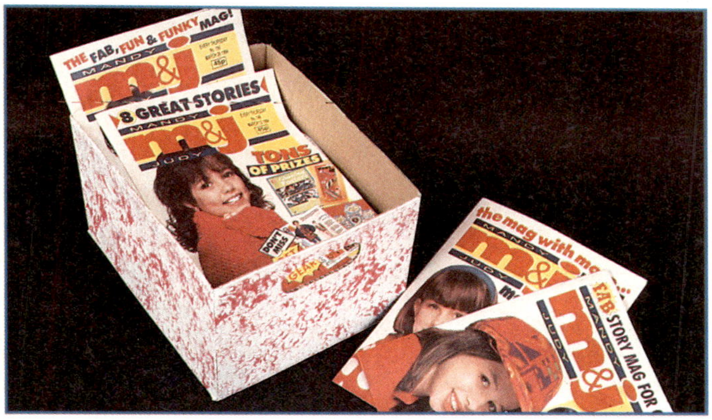

You'll need:- A fairly large cardboard box (the kind that things like kettles and stuff usually come in); some house paint (use left overs or an emulsion sample pot is ideal); bright poster paint; some used Christmas wrap or tissue paper.

What to do:

You can make a boring old box into a mega storage box in minutes. First, cut the top flaps off the box, but DON'T throw them away. Make sure the bottom of the box is secure — you may need to put some glue or tape on it. Paint the box with the emulsion. It won't take long to dry, but you may need two coats — especially if the box has writing on it. You can paint the inside, too, if you like. When the base coat is dry, you can start to decorate.
Mix your poster paint with some water to make it quite thin, but not runny (you won't need a lot of paint). If your base colour is pale, choose a bright contrast, if your base is bright, use a pale contrast. Now for the good bit — crumple up the old wrapping or tissue paper and dip it lightly into the paint. Dab on to your box quickly until it's covered. This gives a crinkly, splash effect. If you want, you can add another colour when the first coat is dry. To finish, cut out some carrying handles. Why not make a set? You can decorate them with different colours and use them to store your 'M&Js', school stuff, books and things.

SEPTEMBER					
S	—	3	10	17	24
M	—	4	11	18	25
Tu	—	5	12	19	26
W	—	6	13	20	27
Th	—	7	14	21	28
F	1	8	15	22	29
S	2	9	16	23	30

OCTOBER					
S	1	8	15	22	29
M	2	9	16	23	30
Tu	3	10	17	24	31
W	4	11	18	25	—
Th	5	12	19	26	—
F	6	13	20	27	—
S	7	14	21	28	—

IMPORTANT DATES ______

NOVEMBER						DECEMBER					
S	—	5	12	19	26	S	—	3	10	17	24/31
M	—	6	13	20	27	M	—	4	11	18	25
Tu	—	7	14	21	28	Tu	—	5	12	19	26
W	1	8	15	22	29	W	—	6	13	20	27
Th	2	9	16	23	30	Th	—	7	14	21	28
F	3	10	17	24	—	F	1	8	15	22	29
S	4	11	18	25	—	S	2	9	16	23	30

Classmates

KIRSTY ALLEN and her classmates were pupils at Tower Hill Comprehensive School. One day, shortly before Christmas —
I'm glad the Head gave us permission to decorate our form rooms, Anita.
Yeah! The place looks great, Kirsty.

There! What do you think of my snowman?
It's brill, Elaine. Looks like our maths teacher, Mr Moore!
Close your eyes, girls! We have a surprise for you!
What is it?
You'll see in a minute!
Ta-ra! MISTLETOE! We'll be all right now, lads! The girls'll be QUEUEING to kiss us under this!
Kiss any of YOU lot? You must be joking!
Yeah! A girl'd have to be DESPERATE!
After school —
MERRY CHRISTMAS
I love Christmas shopping!
Me too! Hey, THAT'S what I want for Christmas — a ghetto-blaster!
I've dropped loads of hints, but I don't know if I'll be lucky. They're dead expensive.
I've asked for some new clothes, but enough about what WE want! We've come to buy presents for other people. What'll I get my gran?
Later —
I've bought everything on my list.
Me, too. Smellies for Mum and Dad, some ace Belgian chocolates for Gran and a musical ball for Sheri. It'll be my first Christmas with my cat. I'm really looking forward to it!

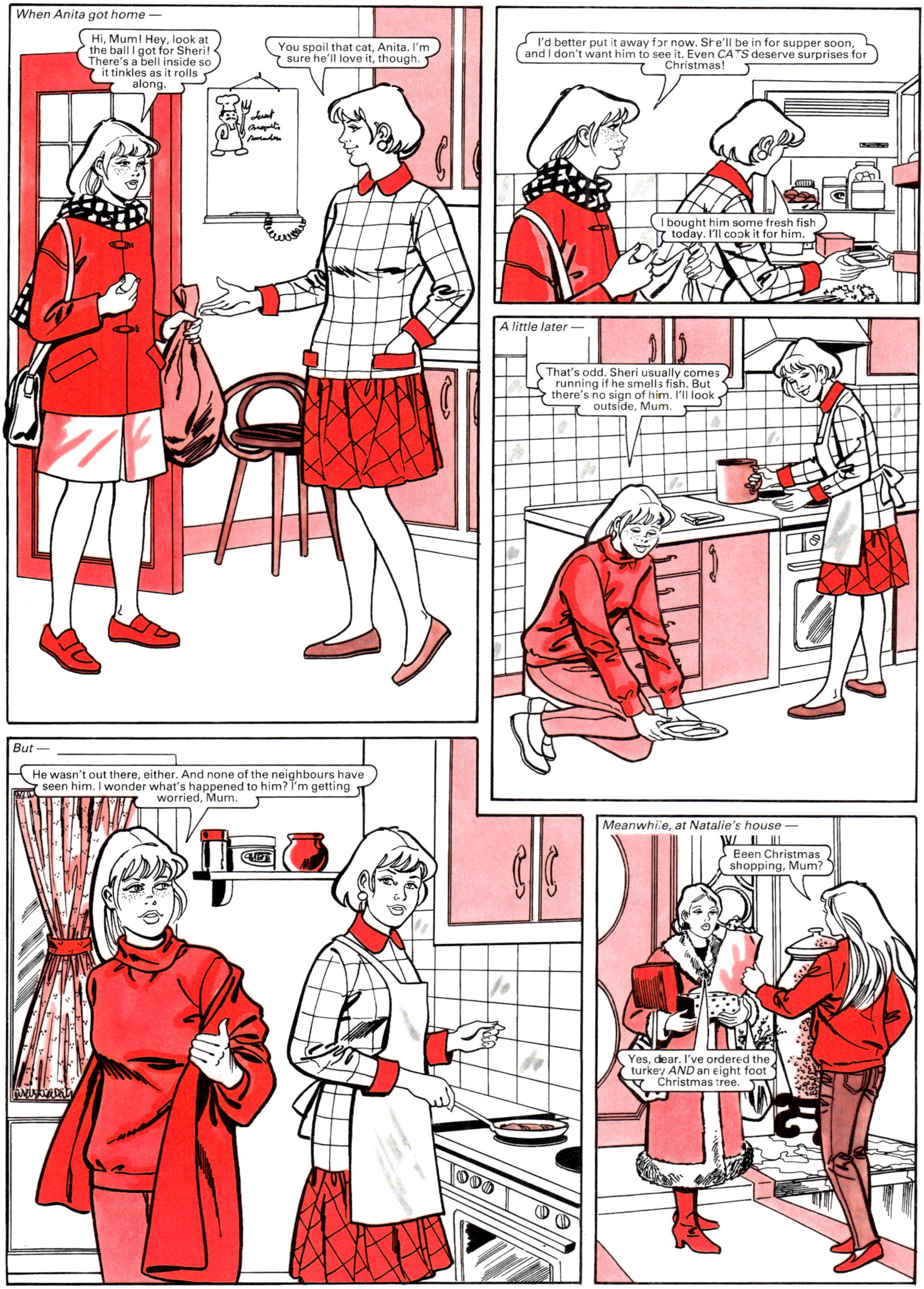

When Anita got home —
Hi, Mum! Hey, look at the ball I got for Sheri! There's a bell inside so it tinkles as it rolls along.
You spoil that cat, Anita. I'm sure he'll love it, though.
I'd better put it away for now. She'll be in for supper soon, and I don't want him to see it. Even CATS deserve surprises for Christmas!
I bought him some fresh fish today. I'll cook it for him.
A little later —
That's odd. Sheri usually comes running if he smells fish. But there's no sign of him. I'll look outside, Mum.
But —
He wasn't out there, either. And none of the neighbours have seen him. I wonder what's happened to him? I'm getting worried, Mum.
Meanwhile, at Natalie's house —
Been Christmas shopping, Mum?
Yes, dear. I've ordered the turkey AND an eight foot Christmas tree.

I said we'd pick up the tree at the weekend.
Great! We're going to have a really TRADITIONAL Christmas — it'll be ace!
Next day, at school —
Kirsty! Something awful's happened!
What is it, Anita?
Sheri's gone missing! He hasn't been seen since yesterday morning. We've searched EVERYWHERE!
Poor Anita. It doesn't sound too good.
Later —
It's rotten seeing Anita so sad before Christmas. If only there was some way I could cheer her up. I know! I could organise a party! I'll ask Mum tonight.
So, later —
A party? I'm not too sure about that, Kirsty.
A few friends round, then — Anita, Jenny and Judith?
Oh — all right.
Next day —
Sheri still hasn't turned up, I'm afraid.
I'm so sorry, Anita. But here's something to take your mind off it. You three are invited to my house on Saturday night.
Ace! From when to when?

Oh! I forgot to agree times with Mum. I'll have to speak to her again tonight.
So —
How late can my friends stay on Saturday, Mum?
Oh, till nine-thirty, dear.
THAT'S not very long!
We do live out of town, so they'll have to travel home, remember. I think nine-thirty is quite late enough.
I don't! We won't be able to fit in half of what I've planned in that short time. Mum won't give in, though.
Meanwhile, at Natalie's —
These Chinese lanterns look lovely! I'm really looking forward to Christmas!
Phone for you, Natalie. It's Dad.
Natalie's parents were divorced —
Hi! Sue and I have decided to go ski-ing in Switzerland over Christmas to a lovely hotel with an indoor pool and its own skating rink. We'd like you to come too Natalie!
Oh! I-I don't know, Dad. I'll have to think about it.

A ski-ing holiday? Well, if you want to go, I'll understand.
It does sound fun. But I fancied a traditional Christmas, too. Oh, now I don't know what to do. How can I choose?
I wish my parents hadn't split up, then I wouldn't BE in this mess.
Next day —
Natalie looks fed-up.
Yes. I don't know why. Anyway, I've spoken to Mum about Saturday. She says the deadline's nine-thirty, unfortunately.
I'm afraid Jenny and I will have to leave even earlier than that. Jenny's parents are out on Saturday so my dad's fetching us both. And he's doing something else after that. He said he'd come at nine o'clock and no later.
Rats! The evening will be REALLY short now!
On Saturday —
I still haven't decided what to do, Mum. A traditional Christmas or a smashing holiday? I just CAN'T choose! I'm sure whichever I pick, I'll wish I'd chosen the other.
It's all right — you don't HAVE to choose. I've spoken to Dad. He's agreed to postpone his trip until Boxing Day. So you can spend a traditional Christmas with me and Ken on the twenty-fifth, and then go ski-ing with Dad and Sue for the rest of the holiday. How does that sound?
Fantastic! THANKS, Mum!
My parents have made sure I WILL have a happy Christmas after all! They're the best Mum and Dad in the world — even if they don't live together any more!
At Kirsty's house —
Hi, you two! Come in out of the rain!
It's awful, isn't it? Imagine having to come to a party in wellies. But we've brought our shoes — and loads of tapes!.
Ace!

But, all too soon —
It's nearly nine o'clock.
Already? Huh! I wanted us to roast chestnuts and tell each other Christmas ghost stories, but there isn't time.
I'd better open the curtains so I can see Dad arriving.
Look! The rain's turned to snow! Wow, it's really thick!
Phone for you, Judith.
It's Dad, saying he might be late. The roads are really treacherous.
Let me speak to him, dear.
I don't want anyone to have an accident. You stay where you are. The girls can sleep here tonight and I'll phone the other parents.
Fantastic! A sleep-over party! Now we WILL have time for all the things I planned!
And, next morning —
That was a super breakfast your mum cooked, Kirsty.
Glad you enjoyed it. Let's take the sledge to the common. There are some great runs there.

This is fun!
Anita STILL looks sad. I feel dead sorry for her. She's really worried about Sheri.
And later, at Anita's —
I know you think Sheri's gone for good, Mum, but I'm going out to search for him again.
All right, dear. Perhaps you'd post these cards for me while you're out.
At the post office —
In they go. Oh! That notice in the window! I don't believe it. I — I think I've found Sheri at last!
Next day —
You've found Sheri? Where was he?
He'd hurt his leg, and a woman took him in and looked after him. She didn't let him out in case he'd open up the wound, which is why he couldn't come home.
But she DID put a notice in the post office window saying she'd found a cat. I knew from the description it was Sheri — and he's safely back with me now!
That's ACE! And hey — guess what? Mum let slip last night that I AM getting a ghetto-blaster for Christmas!
Brill! And look — Natalie's cheered up again, too. I reckon it's going to be a happy Christmas for EVERYONE!
THE END

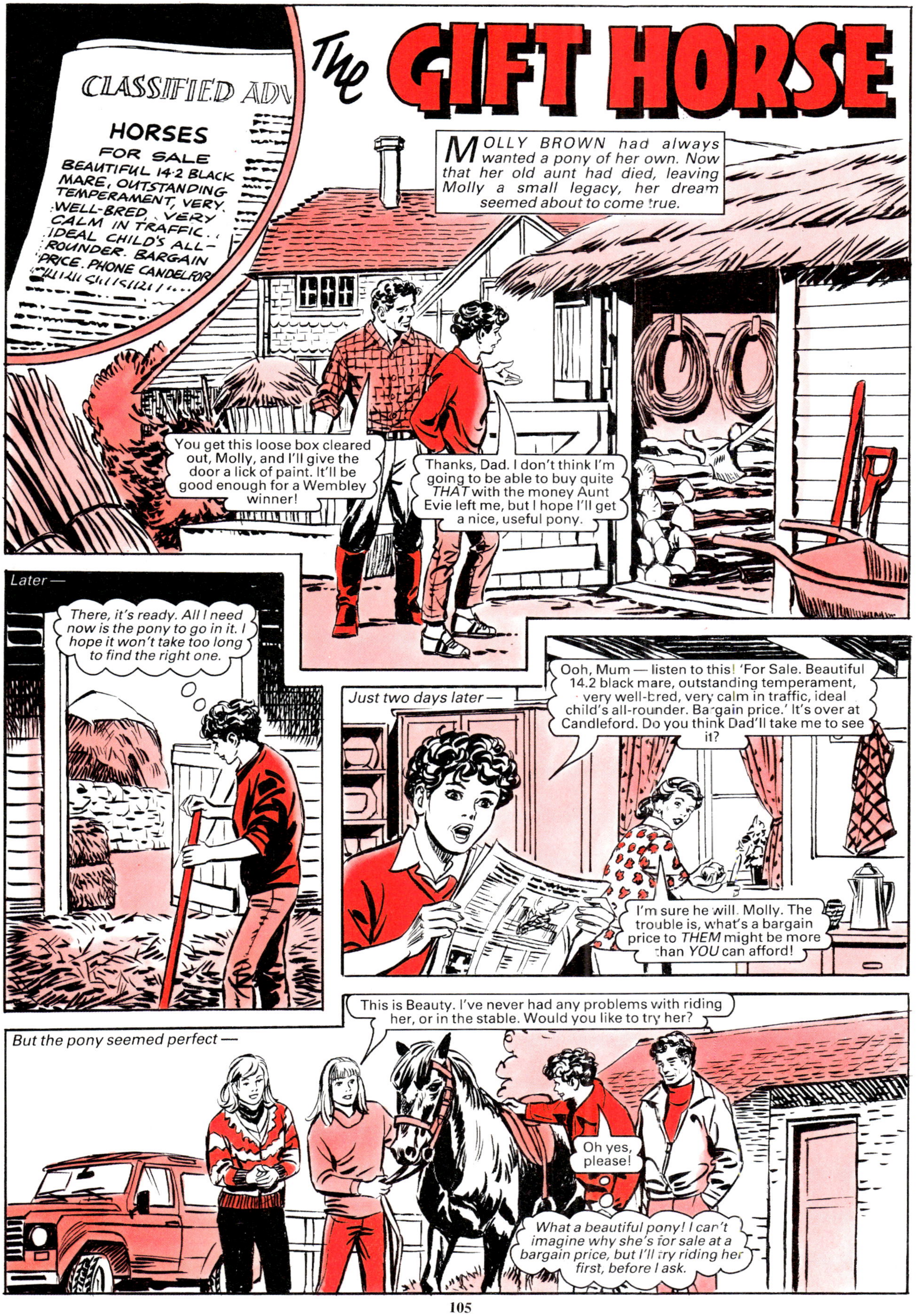
THE GIFT HORSE
CLASSIFIED ADV
HORSES
FOR SALE
BEAUTIFUL 14·2 BLACK MARE, OUTSTANDING TEMPERAMENT, VERY WELL-BRED, VERY CALM IN TRAFFIC. IDEAL CHILD'S ALL-ROUNDER. BARGAIN PRICE. PHONE CANDELFOR
MOLLY BROWN had always wanted a pony of her own. Now that her old aunt had died, leaving Molly a small legacy, her dream seemed about to come true.
You get this loose box cleared out, Molly, and I'll give the door a lick of paint. It'll be good enough for a Wembley winner!
Thanks, Dad. I don't think I'm going to be able to buy quite THAT with the money Aunt Evie left me, but I hope I'll get a nice, useful pony.
Later —
There, it's ready. All I need now is the pony to go in it. I hope it won't take too long to find the right one.
Just two days later —
Ooh, Mum — listen to this! 'For Sale. Beautiful 14.2 black mare, outstanding temperament, very well-bred, very calm in traffic, ideal child's all-rounder. Bargain price.' It's over at Candleford. Do you think Dad'll take me to see it?
I'm sure he will, Molly. The trouble is, what's a bargain price to THEM might be more than YOU can afford!
But the pony seemed perfect —
This is Beauty. I've never had any problems with riding her, or in the stable. Would you like to try her?
Oh yes, please!
What a beautiful pony! I can't imagine why she's for sale at a bargain price, but I'll try riding her first, before I ask.

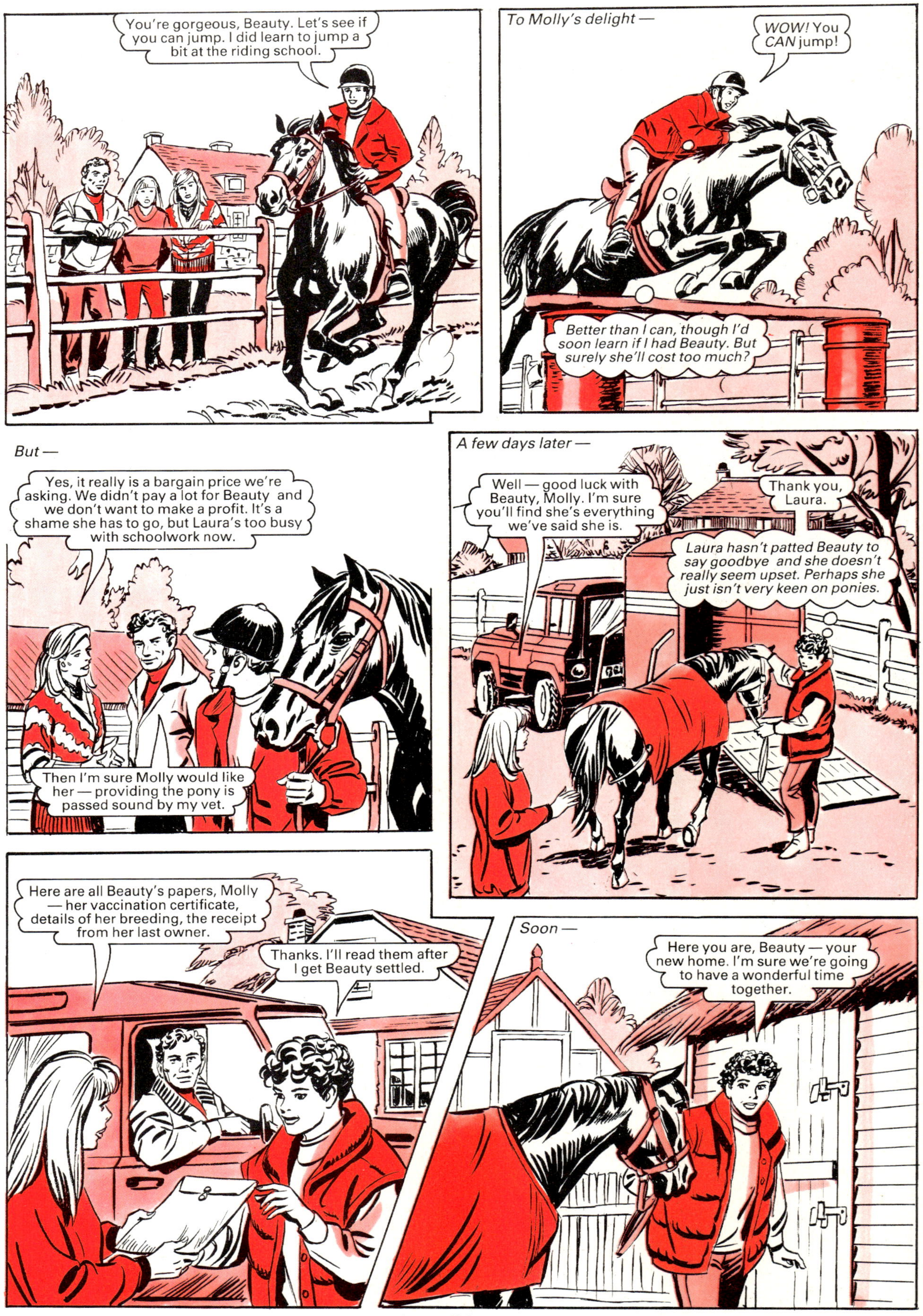
You're gorgeous, Beauty. Let's see if you can jump. I did learn to jump a bit at the riding school.
To Molly's delight —
WOW! You CAN jump!
Better than I can, though I'd soon learn if I had Beauty. But surely she'll cost too much?
But —
Yes, it really is a bargain price we're asking. We didn't pay a lot for Beauty and we don't want to make a profit. It's a shame she has to go, but Laura's too busy with schoolwork now.
Then I'm sure Molly would like her — providing the pony is passed sound by my vet.
A few days later —
Well — good luck with Beauty, Molly. I'm sure you'll find she's everything we've said she is.
Thank you, Laura.
Laura hasn't patted Beauty to say goodbye and she doesn't really seem upset. Perhaps she just isn't very keen on ponies.
Here are all Beauty's papers, Molly — her vaccination certificate, details of her breeding, the receipt from her last owner.
Thanks. I'll read them after I get Beauty settled.
Soon —
Here you are, Beauty — your new home. I'm sure we're going to have a wonderful time together.

Don't you want to explore your stable, Beauty?
Most ponies walk round sniffing and examining everything new, eating hay, trying the water. Beauty just doesn't seem interested, yet she looks perfectly well.
I — I'll be back later, Beauty.
How odd! I feel as if she's WAITING for me to go AWAY. But why?
Later —
Beauty really is well-bred — a thoroughbred cross. All her ancestors are here, right back to Victorian times. There have been several black mares called Beauty — it seems to be a tradition. And there are some newspaper cuttings, too.
Why, this horse of last century looks just like Beauty. Her family must have bred really true to type, all through the generations.
BEAUTY, MISS AMELIA DE VERE'S MARE, AT THE NATIONAL SHOW 1892
Supper, Molly.
Coming, Mum.
There are a few more bits and pieces in here but I'll look at them another time.
After supper —
All right, Beauty? You've eaten your hay, anyway. Don't you want to see if I've got anything for you? All right — I'll come in with your carrot.

BRR! What a cold draught in here! But it isn't a cold night — and — and I almost felt as though there was something behind me. Beauty isn't scared, though.
It's stupid — but I'll be glad to get indoors. Tomorrow, I'll take Beauty for a ride.
Next day —
This is wonderful, Beauty. When we get up onto the open downs, we can have a gallop.
You're really fast, Beauty, but I know I can stop you.
Good girl.
She's lovely — comfortable and responsive. She really WAS a bargain — almost a gift — at the price I paid for her!
Then —
Urgh, what a horrible change in the weather. I can hardly see the path, but YOU can, can't you, Beauty?

I hope this is the right path. Beauty seems quite confident. I know she's new, but Candleford isn't far away. She's probably been up here before.
But —
Beauty — WHOA! Where are we? It — it looks like a steep drop ahead!
A quarry — and we were heading straight for it! But couldn't Beauty sense the drop? Horses usually sense danger.
I'll WALK until I'm sure we're on the right path. That was a narrow escape.
Soon —
That's it — we're almost home now. Never mind, girl. It wasn't your fault.

Oh Beauty, you ARE lovely, yet there's something STRANGE about you. You seem sad and sort of faraway, as if you hardly know I'm here.
That night —
What was that? It sounded like hoofs in the yard.
Someone's riding Beauty! Side-saddle — and — and in strange clothes! I'll wake Dad!
But, in Beauty's stable —
There you are, Molly — your pony's right here. You must have been dreaming.
But, Dad, look! Beauty's sweating — as if she's been ridden.
Next morning —
Dad reckons Beauty was just feeling too warm last night. It certainly seems impossible that I REALLY saw anyone riding her. I'll look up her records. Perhaps one of her previous owners noticed something unusual.

Here's an old print of a girl who looks just like the one I thought I saw riding Beauty — Amelia de Vere. Apparently she went out riding on her black pony, Beauty — and the pony returned alone. Amelia was NEVER seen again!
You're a lovely horse, Beauty, but there's SOMETHING strange about you. Can a horse be HAUNTED, I wonder?
Soon —
Well, that's the deed done. I hate to lose Beauty, but I think I know now why she seemed such a bargain.
ADVERTISING OFFICE
A week later, in a different town —
This sounds like just what I've been looking for, Mum! Look at this advertisement —
HORSES
FOR SALE
BEAUTIFUL 14·2 BLACK MARE.
OUTSTANDING TEMPERAMENT
VERY WELL-BRED VERY CALM IN TRAFFIC. IDEAL CHILD'S ALL-ROUNDER.
BARGAIN PRICE
PHONE
THE END

PUZZLES 'N' THINGS ANSWERS

TRIVIA PUZZLES

PAGE 40

SPORTS — 1. Squash; 2. Tennis; 3. Boxing; 4. Table Tennis; 5. Rugby.

CARTOONS — 1. Bambi; 2. Charlie Brown; 3. Lord Snooty; 4. Mowgli; 5. Cow Pie.

NUMBERS — 1. 13; 2. 11; 3. 12; 4. 101; 5. 3.

ANIMALS — 1. Dog; 2. Horse; 3. Cat; 4. Hedgehog; 5. Zebra.

COLOURS — 1. Green; 2. Blue; 3. Red and white; 4. Black and white; 5. Yellow.

PLACES — 1. Manchester; 2. England; 3. Venice; 4. Ireland; 5. Blackpool.

CROSSWORDS

PAGE 44

Across: 1. Buttercup 5. Snap 7. Stow 8. Toot 10. Heart 13. Liar 14. Trek 15. Eiderdown.
Down: 1. Bask 2. That 3. Cut 4. Paws 6. Poker 7. Start 9. Clue 10. Hand 11. Trio 12. Skin.

Across: 3. Limit 5. Nurse 6. Niece 8. Finest 12. Simple 15. Water 16. Ocean 17. Lemon.
Down: 1. Knife 2. Wren 3. Lens 4. Inc 7. Item 9. Ease 10 Beans 11. Case 13. Iron 14. Prey.

ON THE BOX

PAGE 87

1. Saffron; 2. Nicholas Lyndhurst; 3. Pugsley; 4. 90210; 5. Bayside; 6. Dean Cain; 7. Gladiators; 8. a) Matt Brody, b) Mitch Buchanan; 9. Coronation Street; 10. 7 a.m.; 11. Sharon (Pauline Quirke) Tracey (Linda Robson); 12. Krypton; 13. Dawn French; 14. a) The Flintstones, b) Bugs Bunny, c) Scooby Doo; 15. Alexei Sayle; 16. The Man From U.N.C.L.E; 17. Lassie; 18. Maureen; 19. Fred Savage; 20. Home And Away.

ALPHABET QUIZ

PAGE 89

A Ace; B Big Daddy's; C Chesterfield; D Dogs; E Elephant; F February; G Georgie Porgy; H Heffalumps; I Incy Wincy; J Jason Donovan; K Ken; L Leather; M Mistletoe; N Nicola Stapleton; O Oak; P Phillip Schofield; Q Quack; R Roger the Dodger; S Superman; T Tennis; U U.S.A.; V Valentine cards; W Washington D.C.; X X-ray; Y Yolk; Z Zebra.

READY, STEADY GO!

PAGE 90

1. Gary Barlow, Jason Orange, Howard Donald, Mark Owen and Robbie Williams; 2. Home & Away; 3. 2 Unlimited; 4. Arnold Schwarzenneger; 5. Craig McLachlan; 6. The Addams Family; 7. Mrs Doubtfire; 8. Mayim Bialik; 9. 4; 10. Zig and Zag; 11. Mr Blobby; 12. Summer Bay; 13. Gladiators; 14. It's part of the postcode of the area they live in; 15. Beauty And The Beast; 16. Bjorn Again; 17. Bill and Ted; 18. Joey Lawrence; 19. Becky and Darlene; 20. Take That; 21. Dean Cain; 22. Grange Hill; 23. The cookery bit; 24. Edd on CBBC; 25. Lulu; 26. Kylie and Dannii; 27. Fighter pilot; 28. Will Smith; 29. Lost in New York; 30. A St Bernard dog.

DO THEY DIFFER?

PAGE 92

1. Door handle; 2. Extra line on fire place; 3. Extra bit on pencil; 4. Writing on note pad; 5. Spot on dog; 6. Snowman's nose; 7. Snowman's arm; 8. Extra button on snowman; 9. Seagull on painting; 10. Bauble on fireplace; 11. Bauble on fireplace; 12. Design on fireguard extra; 13. Green ball of wool; 14. Bone on floor; 15. Design on chair in other room; 16. Extra Xmas card on door; 17. Small painting on wall; 18. Small painting on wall; 19. Sun in painting; 20. Extra bauble on Xmas tree.

NURSES
VERITY, Amanda, Jackie, Kay and Chris were first-year nursing students at Norchester General Hospital, and shared a house together. One day, Amanda was working on the children's ward —
Meet Julie and her mother, Nurse Bailey.
Hello, Julie.
She's the little girl who's being admitted for a very serious operation.
This is your bed. I'll have to fill in an identification bracelet for you. What's your full name?
Julie Ann Kershaw. Why do I have to wear that?
So that every nurse and doctor who sees you knows who you are. A lot of the things we do here might seem a bit strange, but don't worry! You'll be up and out of hospital again in no time.
I know. I have to get well soon — for Skipper's sake. Skipper's my dog. Like to see his photo?
Skipper loves me a lot and I love him. He'll be missing me while I'm away, so I promised him I'd soon be home with him.
That's nice.
Meanwhile, Kay was working on a women's ward —
Nurse Baxter! Time to do the drugs round!
I wish Sister Lawler wouldn't YELL! She's got a voice like a FOG-HORN!!

Next morning —
It's Julie's operation today.
Is that the little girl with the dog?
She's bound to be a bit nervous, poor kid.
Verity's right. But I've had an idea.
When the hospital porters arrived to take Julie to the theatre —
Ready, Julie?
NO! I don't want to go, nurse!
It's all right. There's no need to worry. Skipper's coming, too!
The dog?
No, his photo! You hold Skipper tightly, Julie, and don't let him fall off the bed. He'll watch over you during the operation.
They'll give her an injection to make her unconscious. Once she's asleep, I'll whip away the photo and take it back to her locker in the ward so that it's the first thing she sees when she comes round.
That evening —
Phew! What a day! Sister Lawler bawled at me non-stop!
I've heard she can be a real battle-axe.
I'm tired out too. Let's have an early night.
But the girls hadn't been asleep for long when —
Kay! Amanda! Wake up! I think we're being BURGLED! There's someone scuffling about outside the back door!
What? I'll call the police.

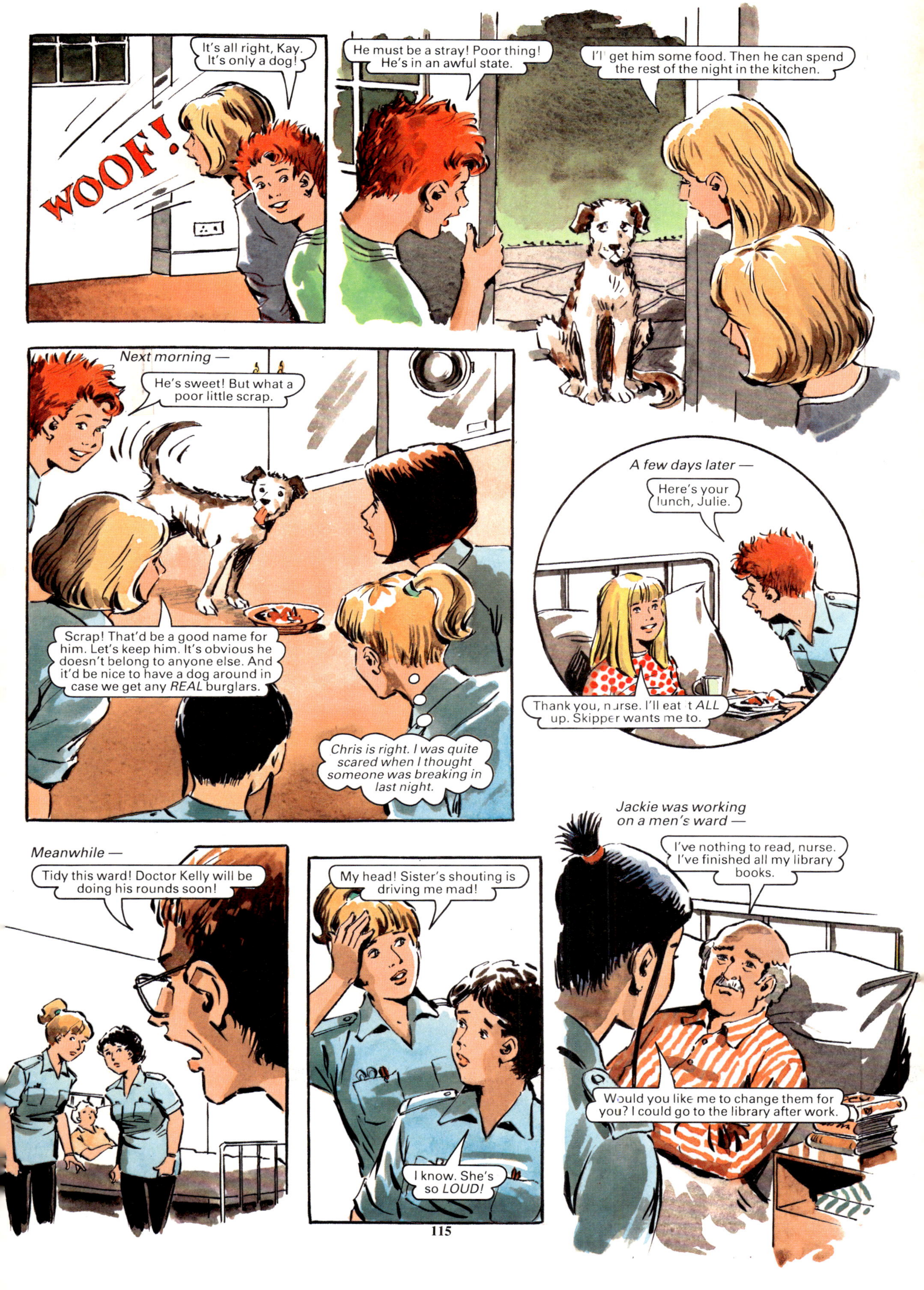

WOOF!
It's all right, Kay. It's only a dog!
He must be a stray! Poor thing! He's in an awful state.
I'll get him some food. Then he can spend the rest of the night in the kitchen.
Next morning —
He's sweet! But what a poor little scrap.
Scrap! That'd be a good name for him. Let's keep him. It's obvious he doesn't belong to anyone else. And it'd be nice to have a dog around in case we get any REAL burglars.
Chris is right. I was quite scared when I thought someone was breaking in last night.
A few days later —
Here's your lunch, Julie.
Thank you, nurse. I'll eat it ALL up. Skipper wants me to.
Meanwhile —
Tidy this ward! Doctor Kelly will be doing his rounds soon!
My head! Sister's shouting is driving me mad!
I know. She's so LOUD!
Jackie was working on a men's ward —
I've nothing to read, nurse. I've finished all my library books.
Would you like me to change them for you? I could go to the library after work.

And so —
Hi, Amanda! I'm late 'cos I had to go to the library. It was my turn to take Scrap for a walk, too, so I hope someone else has.
But —
Oh, no! All the others must be late home, too. Scrap's *STILL* shut in and he doesn't like it one little bit!
HOWL!
Oh, dear! The neighbours will soon complain if he keeps making a noise like that.
Next day —
That's it, Julie — one step at a time. You'll soon be out taking Skipper for walks!
Mrs Kershaw looks anxious. Maybe she doesn't realise how well Julie's progressing. I'll have a word with her.
. . . so there's really no need to worry.
But there *IS!* It's *SKIPPER!* He was pining for Julie and when my husband let him out one night, he ran off! We've looked *EVERYWHERE,* but we can't find him. How can I tell Julie?
Next morning —
Good morning, Staff. Where's Sister Lawler?
She hasn't turned up! She must be off sick. Peace and quiet at last! That means I'm in charge for the moment. I've just had a call from Casualty. They're sending us a patient. We'd better make up a bed. It'll be great! No-one to bawl at us as we work!
But then —
Here comes the new patient. Oh, no! I don't *BELIEVE* it!
Sister Lawler! Looks as if she's broken her leg. She must have done it on her way to work.

Soon —
NURSE! Fetch me a cup of tea! And this bed needs tidying!
Would you believe it? Sister's off sick, but she's STILL bawling at us!
On the children's ward, it was visiting time —
Our next door neighbour's here to see you, Julie.
Hello, love. I've brought you a doll to cuddle. I thought it might make up a bit for losing Skipper.
Oh, no! The neighbour didn't realise it was supposed to be a SECRET!
From then on —
I'm very worried. Julie's not progressing like she should.
She seems to have lost the will to get better, doctor.
And we all know why! It's such a shame.
Later —
Scrap's been chewing the furniture. Don't think he likes being left at home alone all day. I guess it's not fair to have a pet when we're all working. Maybe we ought to find him a new home.
A new home? That gives me an idea!
Next day —
The doctor's ordered Julie to sit outside in the sun. He thinks it might aid her recovery. So here goes —
Julie! I've brought something to show you.
This is Scrap! He needs a new home. Would you like to look after him?
What a wonderful idea, Julie! He could take Skipper's place.
No! Scrap's a nice dog, but I want Skipper! He's the ONLY dog for me!

On Saturday —
Julie didn't want Scrap and WE can't keep him. We'll have to take him to the dogs' home.
They'll find an owner who'll care for him.
And so —
Bring the little fellow this way. He's lovely — we'll have no trouble finding him a good home.
There are lots of strays here.
Then —
Oh, I know THAT dog! It's SKIPPER! I recognise him from his photo!
Skipper had been found wandering a few days before —
I'm delighted you know the owner, dear!
I'll take him straight to the hospital.
And —
Skipper! You've come back!
Look at her face! Julie will start recovering again now. I can't thank you enough, dear.
No problem, Mrs Kershaw! It's all part of a nurse's work!
THE END

m&j
JUDY JONES and Mandy Taylor were best friends who lived next door to each other. One day, during the Christmas holidays . . .
Brr! It's really cold. But it hasn't snowed yet, Mandy. Think of the fun we could have if it did — snowballing, sledging . . .
. . . or skating or building a snowman. I wish the snow WOULD come!
Next morning—
Brill! The snow's here at last. It'll be ace to play in! I'll go round for Mandy straight after breakfast.
But—
I'm sorry, Judy — Mandy's not here. She and Patch went to her aunt's in Milchester last night, and when it started snowing, Uncle Des insisted she stayed overnight. Now she won't be able to get back until it thaws.
OH, NO!
Oh, rats! Now the snow's finally here, we can't be together to enjoy it. I'll just have to play by myself.
Snowballing's no fun when you've no-one to aim at. Maybe skating would be better . . .

The flooded meadow's frozen over! That's a safe place to skate . . .
. . . if only I could stay upright. I need a friend to cling on to. Skating's hopeless on your own!
I know! I'll build a snowman! But instead of being just an ordinary man, it can be a model of Mandy and Patch! That should cheer me up!
But—
This is no good! It looks nothing like Mandy or Patch.
I might as well give up.
Then—
AAH! Who threw that?

There's nobody there except the model Mandy and Patch — and snowmen can't throw snowballs!
Don't go, Judy!
Eh? That was Mandy's voice!
It's as if my model's alive!
Of course it isn't! It's *ME!*
MANDY!
The road from Milchester has been cleared by a snowplough, so I came home! I wanted to play in the snow with you.
You'd better watch out! I've loadsa snowballs here!
Aah! I'll get you, Mandy Taylor! And when we've finished here, we can go skating! This is more like it!
THE END

Skeleton Corner

Don't you know the legend about the little hill in the field out there? If you see the Snow People, who are like ELVES, dancing on it in the snow after dark on Christmas Eve, you can make a wish. And your wish will come true!
Well, no sign of snow, so we've had THAT. But don't you get a wish with your first mince pie?
That's not your first! THIRTIETH, more like!
A little later—
I'm off to bed now.
I want to be fresh tomorrow in case Stephen DOES come. That'd be a BRILL present!
But Esme didn't sleep well—
Two o'clock. Hey, it's dead quiet.
It's snowing, but I don't see any Snow People dancing on the hill. Pity, 'cos I know what I'd have wished for—
—to see Stephen!
A couple of hours later Esme woke again. And THIS time—
Th-the Snow People! D-dancing—just like the legend said!

Esme watched for ages —
Oh! I'm enjoying this so much that I haven't made my wish yet! I'll do it now!
Seconds later—
They've gone! Just VANISHED!
Not many hours later—
Goodness! You're an early bird, dear.
I thought I'd help you with the preparations, Gran.
And I don't want to miss Stephen!
But, as the morning went on—
See what I got, Sally!
Sounds like the others are getting up. And looks like the Grays AREN'T coming.
Even though I saw the Snow People dancing AND made a wish!
Unhappily, Esme went outside—
Huh — there's NO snow anywhere! I must have DREAMT the Snow People!

Shame! And not just 'cos of the wish but 'cos such a lovely experience was only a dream!
Back inside, Esme tried to cheer up —
I bet you two DIDN'T manage to stay awake last night.
We DID!
We didn't see Santa, though. But we saw people dancing on the hill—
Were they carol singers or something, Esme? They were dead funny-looking.
Yeah — like ELVES!
They CAN'T be making this up, 'cos they were in bed when Gran told us about the legend.
Just then, the doorbell rang, and—
Hello! We're a lot later than we intended. Trouble with the car in the snow. I know we're only ten miles away, but it's deep where we are — though you don't have any.
Hi, Esme! I hoped I'd see you — despite the snow!
Oh, there WAS some snow in the night, but it's melted. It wasn't much, you see —
— but it was ENOUGH! I DIDN'T dream the Snow People after all! I DID see them — and they made my Christmas wish come true!
THE END

Wish Upon A Star

Ah, what a glamorous life those pop and film peeps live, eh, girls? Or do they?

Take That — the lurvliest boys on earth . . .

. . . but would you fancy them in this lot? Those ba[illegible] trews, that spiky hair, t[illegible] HEADBAND! Call t[illegible] fashion polic[illegible]

Christian Slater's a v. handsome young heart-throb, isn't he?

Except when he's impersonating a tramp, that is!